As a pastor and father of two [barcode D0993188] d with joy for you to learn about this moven Matthew and Terah have been an inspiration and encouragement from day one. Their story is a story of faith, trust, disappointment and courage. But above all it is God's story. You will be challenged and inspired as you read about this journey. You will see how God can move if you allow Him access to your heart and mind. You will be challenged to look deep into your own walk with God. So be ready to experience mission and purpose like never before. I've so enjoyed being a part of this journey and can't wait to see what God has in store for you and Psalm 82:3.

—Matthew Craig,
Lead Pastor, First Christian Church of Scottsburg

An honest and practical look at the highs and lows of Kingdom work, Lee's story is a wonderful reminder of God's bigger plans being revealed to those who faithfully follow Christ's call. An encouragement for anyone in the midst of an unsettled ministry season.

—Patrick Snow,
Vice President of Content, Christ in Youth

I've had the privilege of knowing Matt for the last decade and his story for Psalm 82:3, printed here in the pages of *Faith Steps*, is as inspiring to me today as the first day our church joined in to support the mission in Liberia. There is no question that you will be inspired by his level of faith and dedication to the mission God has given him to 'defend the weak and the fatherless and uphold the cause of the poor and the oppressed.' The question will be what you choose to do in response to that inspiration!

—Jason Rehmel,
Lead Pastor, Eastside Christian Church, Milford, OH

As someone who has spent just about my entire life in one place, reading about Matt's experiences opens my eyes up to the great work the Lord is doing across the globe, in places and in lives much different from my own. We need to be regularly shaken out of our ethnocentric tunnel-vision and reminded of the global body of Christ.

—John Davis,
Pastor, and author of *God-Centered Christianity*

Matthew shares his journey in a way that feels utterly accessible and replicable. Sometimes in this space, the steps towards adoption and orphan and vulnerable children advocacy seem complicated, and thus unattainable. The Lees allow us to see inside their family and track their growth and learnings. This kind of access invites risk, and is a gift to the entire community. Enjoy!

—Beth Guckenberger,
Co-Executive Director, Back2Back Ministries,
adoptive and foster mom, author

Psalm 37:23 says, "The steps of a good man are ordered by the Lord: and he delighteth in his way." In this book, Matthew Lee shares the steps that he and his family have taken in their amazing God-adventure. This is a book I wish I had read earlier in my Christian life. You'll be challenged and inspired in your own walk with the Lord!

—Ryan Frank,
CEO/Publisher at KidzMatter

We are told in the Bible that we "walk by faith, not by sight." In this wonderful book, you will truly see a person who lived this out with his family. You will be reminded that God is in the details of our lives, even in the seasons of extended waiting. I was inspired by this powerful story and I know you will be, too!

—Greg Horn,
Executive Director, HOPE is Here Ministries

God is able "to do more than all we ask or imagine." Matt Lee and his family are a great example of this. As they made themselves available and put their faith in Him, God in His power worked through them to create an incredible, life-changing ministry. This book will encourage, inspire, and challenge you to do the same.

—Chip West,
Pastor, Main Street Christian Church, Rushville, Indiana

How do we put the words of Jesus Christ in Matthew 25 and 28 into action? In Matthew 25, Jesus separates the sheep from the goats based upon their actions to help the less fortunate in His kingdom. In Matthew 25:42-43, Jesus says, "For I was hungry and you gave me nothing to eat, I was thirsty and you gave me nothing to drink, I was a stranger and you did not invite me in, I needed clothes and you did not clothe me, I was sick and in prison and you did not look after me."

But Jesus tells us to do more than help people physically. Jesus says in Matthews 28:19-20 to make disciples and grow His kingdom with new believers: "Therefore go and make disciples of all nations, baptizing them in the name of the Father and of the Son and of the Holy Spirit, and teaching them to obey everything I have commanded you. And surely I am with you always, to the very end of the age."

Faith Steps tells the story of Psalm 82:3 following the words of Jesus in Matthew 25 and 28. From a modest beginning, the work of Psalm 82:3 has been greatly blessed by the Lord. This is not to the glory of the Psalm 82:3 staff—it is to the glory of the Father. In fact, Jesus promises this in John 15:7-8: "If you remain in me and my words remain in you, ask whatever you wish, and it will be done for you. This is to my Father's glory, that you bear much fruit, showing yourselves to be my disciples."

Faith Steps sums it up best: "The journey of Psalm 82:3 Mission continues to take steps to develop a safe children's village and self-sustainable community center in Liberia, Africa. Each day lives are impacted through foster care, church and community, medical care, education, and employment. The commitment to defend the weak and fatherless deepens daily as one of the poorest places on planet earth becomes a place of hope, healing, and brighter futures."

Jesus tells us that if we follow His commands, we are considered His friends. The staff of Psalm 82:3 are friends of Jesus. John 15:14-15 says, "You are my friends if you do what I command. I no longer call you servants because a servant does not know his master's business. Instead, I have called you friends, for everything that I learned from my Father I have made known to you."

—Dr. Greg Kasten,
Tates Creek Christian Elder and U.S. Board Member

Without faith, it is impossible to please him. What a beautiful story of faith! Matt takes you on an inspiring and heartfelt journey as he and his family take a trust fall into God's plan over their own. We don't always have the answers, but we can trust that God does and that He will make a way as we trust Him with our stories. This book will ignite your faith and challenge you to return to your first love and trust him again like never before."

—Esther Moreno,
Founder, Child's Heart LLC

For foreign and subsidiary rights, contact the author.

Cover design by: Sara Young

Cover photo by: Amy Barrentine Photography
Author photo on cover: Amy Barrentine Photography

ISBN: 978-1-957369-48-8   1 2 3 4 5 6 7 8 9 10

Printed in the United States of America

FAITH STEPS

THE PSALM 82:3 MISSION STORY

MATTHEW LEE

KUDU

DEDICATION

For the defenders of the fatherless and vulnerable
children of our world . . . keep defending!

ACKNOWLEDGMENTS

To the team at Kudu Publishing, Four Rivers Media, and my friend John Schondelmayer, thank you for your guidance to putting *Faith Steps* into book form.

To my friends, Mark Hester, Wayne Kramer, and many others, for your in-depth proofreading. Thank you for cleaning up my mumbles and making them understandable.

To those I have had the honor to serve in ministry with, walk life with, and follow Christ with, thank you for being the iron that sharpened my iron. Your friendships are a rare treasure that I hold dear.

To every mission team partner, fellow adoptive family, and Psalm 82:3 Mission Defender locally, globally, past, present, and future, the dream continues. Together, we defend like champions!

To my siblings, parents, and in-laws, you have constantly nudged me forward when it would have been much easier to let me wander off the trail like a lost cowboy. Thank you for not giving up, pushing me to try again, and giving me the freedom to grow in Christ in my own unique way. You taught me at an early age to listen closely for the still, small voice of the Holy Spirit in the midst of all the noise. I am still learning to listen.

Never last, and always most important on this earth—To my bonita Terah, sons Colten and Onah, and daughters Blessing, Marie, and Izzy, your ability to love me in my weakest moments, breathe encouragements on my hardest days, and make endless sacrifices in this faith journey inspire me daily to be a better example of Jesus, a better husband, and a better father. Thank you for trusting me to lead our family and for taking every step together!

Contents

Dedication vii

Acknowledgments ix

Introduction: *Steps Toward Home* 13

CHAPTER 1. **Baby Steps** 17

CHAPTER 2. **Trust Me. Test Me.** 23

CHAPTER 3. **If God . . .** 31

CHAPTER 4. **Pigs, Cans, and Provisions** 37

CHAPTER 5. **Transformation** 43

CHAPTER 6. **FinaLee Home** 49

CHAPTER 7. **Ice Cream Sundae** 57

CHAPTER 8. **Choosing to Defend** 65

CHAPTER 9. **Hold on Tight** 71

CHAPTER 10. **Unexpected Blessings** 79

CHAPTER 11. **Trust and Obey** 87

Conclusion: *A Few More Steps to Home* 95

STEPS TOWARD HOME

The year before my wife, Terah, and I began dating, a colt named Chance was born on my parent's farm. It was our job to train him to ride. Nearly every time we were home from college, we went for a ride and continued to train him. After college, we were married—we made sure that Chance was a part of our wedding as we rode off into the sunset. A couple of years later, we moved Chance from my parent's farm to a friend's farm on the opposite side of the city, where we lived. The next year, we bought an old farmhouse next to an overgrown farm. We received permission to put up a fence so that Chance could move next door to our house. We made a few adjustments to our detached two-car garage, which included adding a small side entrance door and turning one bay into a horse stall. Finally, it was time to bring Chance to our home.

Enjoying the journey and an opportunity to spend the day in nature, I took a quick glance at a map and decided to ride Chance from our friend's farm to our house. I estimated that the entire twelve-mile ride should take three to four hours and was basically a straight path along the river from one side of the county to the other. I waited for the perfect weather day, packed my lunch, saddled my horse, and began the journey home.

Shortly into the ride, I realized this journey would be longer than expected and harder than I had hoped. At first, I realized my miscalculation: the river was farther away than I thought, and reaching it would entail passing a field of nearly fifty recently-groomed and curious alpacas that ran toward us. These creatures, that looked like long-legged poodles with lion's manes, scared Chance, which threw us into a full-fledged sprint of terror. By the time we stopped running, I had lost my lunch. Not in a sick way—I literally lost my sack lunch. An hour later, we reached the edge of the river, both horse and rider covered in sweat.

The river was cool, calm, and appeared to be mostly shaded, which should have made for a simple ride home from that point. A few steps into the water, though, new realities were realized. The river was flowing in the opposite direction than we were headed, and it was quite deep in many places. To add to these facts, nearly every grassy space well-suited for taking a break was someone's backyard. My trusted steed and I traveled on. Sometimes, I would get off and walk along with Chance to give him a break and stretch my legs. For more than three hours, we walked against the river. When we reached the edge of the city, I hoped that only a few more steps through town would lead us to the home stretch of this already long journey.

In Hebrews 11:1 (NIV), the author states, "Now faith is confidence in what we hope for and assurance about what we do not see."

Throughout the next few pages, I hope to share with you about a journey that my family began in 2007—a journey that has guided us through three international adoptions, starting non-profit organizations in two countries, and developing a growing ministry more than 6,000 miles away. Every step has grown our faith, and without each step, the next step would not have been possible. Each day, we become more confident that God will make a way—that He alone will guide us through, and that His name will be glorified.

My hope for you, reader, is that you will be able to insert your faith story into the pages of this story. I hope that you will identify the step you are on and decide to take one more step forward in trusting the Author of each of our stories.

CHAPTER 1

BABY STEPS

n the Neekreen District, Grand Bassa County, Liberia, Africa, a 50-acre tract of land is being transformed into a safe children's village and a self-sustainable community center. The land that was dense forest in April 2018 is now a foster care village, a school, a medical clinic, a church, and an agriculture development. Beyond the land, hundreds of vulnerable children are served weekly, prisoners are taught the truth of God's Word, and villages are finding help. The land has been set apart to defend the weak and the fatherless and is overseen by a team of people that call themselves "Defenders."

Through the love of Jesus, many lives are finding hope every day.

That is where this story continues, but it is not where the story began.

In the life of a child, the transition from crawling to walking doesn't happen immediately. After learning to crawl, a determination arises in the child to reach for new things and a confidence grows in his or her newfound abilities. The child begins taking chances to reach what is possible, while not stepping away fully from what they depend on. Finally, the day comes for the child to take a step. Putting a couple of these steps together, the child can eventually walk across the room. These steps soon lead to running, climbing, jumping, and much more. The child has begun their steps toward independence.

My parents—my father a minister and my mother a teacher—built a solid faith foundation for my two older brothers, my younger sister, and me. We were at nearly every church event or program. Family vacations were often connected to special conferences, and our lives were centered around things like church camp, large dinners, revival services, church musicals, and Vacation Bible School. If it was something designed to draw us closer to Jesus, we were probably participating. When we were not at church events, our parents were transporting us from sport to sport, or we were working on our family farm. Regardless of what we were doing, we rarely missed a Sunday gathering with the church.

When I was a baby, my parents chose to dedicate my life to full-time church ministry. The choice to stay on this path would always be mine, but I always loved learning about and doing ministry. I would often take notes from my father's sermons to preach to my younger sister each Sunday. In fact, my father even built a little wooden stand for me to preach from and a bench for my sister to sit on. Special groups—like puppet ministry, special needs ministry, a southern bluegrass band, and caroling at nursing homes—were some of my favorites. The church was my second home.

At nine years old, my father's role as lead minister transitioned our family from Kent, Indiana, to Arlington, Indiana. With the many unknowns of life ahead, I wanted to remember my Kent church family as my home church by making the decision to follow Jesus and be baptized.

One of the hardest challenges of maintaining a garden is preventing the weeds from growing. It seems that weeds, like thistles, are the hardest to prevent and nearly impossible to get rid of in a garden. The reality of the weed is that if the root is not dug out entirely, the damage it does under the surface is far greater than what is seen above the ground.

Like most new Christians, I was enthusiastic about Christ in the beginning. Nothing had changed in my family's commitment to being at church; but after a few years, my fire of faith faded to burning embers. I allowed myself to explore temptations like cursing and, at twelve years old, began a long journey battling a hidden sin that remained with me into young adulthood.

Throughout high school, I participated in theater, choir, soccer, swimming, and my church youth group. It was through the youth group that I met my wife, Terah. We had the typical boy-girl relationship: boy meets girl. Boy annoys girl. Girl rejects boy until girl finally agrees to spend time with boy as friends. Boy adores girl. Girl realizes boy isn't going away. The rest is history.

Toward the end of my senior year of high school, my family's time of serving in full-time church ministry ended abruptly. This gave me the excuse I needed to forego the plan of going into full-time ministry and instead look at another career option in telecommunications. In these moments, I was convinced that I could continue down the path of my own sins and spiritual disconnectedness, while also pretending to be a follower of Jesus.

Nearly halfway into my freshman year at a private college, I knew I wasn't on the right path. I never went off the path, but I'd certainly hit the guardrails many times. One night, I was meeting with one of my dorm counselors and sharing about where I was at in life. He challenged me to submit to what God was leading me toward—the calling He'd given me. After my conversation with my counselor, I prayed. It was probably my first real prayer in a long time, and it was simple: "God, I know you want me to go into full-time ministry, but I don't want to do that. I am willing to obey you Lord, but you are going to have to make it happen. Amen."

I soon received a call from a lady in my hometown who was trying to get a youth ministry going in her rural church. She knew my parents well and wondered if I would be interested in being the youth minister. There would be no interview and the job would be mine if I wanted it. My response was quick: "No, thank you." So much for submitting fully to God's plans, huh? But this did become a turning point toward God's direction—it led me to change colleges and majors at the end of my freshman year. I transferred to the same university Terah was attending to join her in focusing on Elementary Education. In my mind and heart, I was being obedient to God . . . on my own terms.

Attending college together allowed Terah and I to connect to a couple different college groups both on and off campus. We began attending the weekly Fellowship of Christian Athletes group on campus. Toward the end of the fall semester of our sophomore year, an opportunity to serve at a church camp in the mountains outside Tegucigalpa, Honduras, was offered for the following spring break. Over the next few months, I planned and prepared for my first mission trip with a group of people that had become acquaintances of mine.

Arriving in Honduras was similar to a trip to Mexico I had taken with my high school choir; but the arrival at the church camp was like a different world altogether. The camp was nestled in the middle of five mountain peaks, and the houses around it were nearly all broken down. Still, the joy found in nearly every person was unmistakable. I enjoyed the idea of adventure as I looked at each mountain peak and saw a daily challenge. I set my internal alarm for 5:00 a.m. to hike to the top of a peak before the team breakfast. The journey to the top the next morning was rather simple, but when I reached the summit, I could see for miles. Standing at the mountain's edge, the fresh air filled my lungs. For a moment, I felt like I could reach out and touch heaven. Overwhelmed by the sight around me, my mouth soon opened and songs I remembered from my youth flowed freely from my lips. For the first time in a long time, my worship was pure and focused on God. I spent some time in prayer and study and then returned to camp shortly after the breakfast meeting.

Throughout the rest of our journey in Honduras, it seemed like my time to the mountain peak became an invitation for others to join. Each day, new team members would wake up early with me and set out for another day of discovery, worship, and time alone with God. By the end of the week, nearly the entire team—including the camp director—was making the trek to the top of the mountain. At the end of one of our hikes, I finally asked the camp director a question that had been burning inside of me all week. All week, I had watched this man bounce out of his own broken-down house ready to meet the day, like Tigger from Winnie the Pooh, while I often struggled to get to my feet because of the day ahead. Sleep wasn't easy at this camp, as we each took our place on a concrete floor with a mosquito net draped across two chairs.

Through a translator, I asked the camp director, "How do you greet each day with such joy in the midst of such hardship?"

He replied with a smile. "I feel sorry for Americans. You come here with so much physical stuff in your life that you don't remember this world is not your home. It's just temporary. For me, I know that each new day is one step closer to home. That makes me excited."

I wish I could say that the trip to Honduras was the moment I left behind my hidden sin, or even the moment I fully surrendered to God in full-time ministry. I can't, though. I wasn't there yet in my journey; but something had begun to awaken in me. The once-burning embers had been joined with a fresh log of faith and the fire had begun to burn again.

When I returned from Honduras, I received another call from the same person as the previous year offering me the youth ministry job. This time, I accepted the position and began traveling back home every weekend to serve the youth of this church. For the next year and a half, the Lord used this church filled with simplicity to rebuild my soul and excite me for possibilities. From harvest parties and pool parties to having so much fun in kids' worship that I literally split my pants, this church became a place of healing for me.

Each of these steps were like baby steps of faith. To see what God had next in my life, I had to be willing to submit to His leading. I had to be willing to trust Him in uncomfortable situations and experience faith from a mountain-view experience. Eventually, a few of these steps blended together, and instead of depending on my parents' faith, I began to take steps toward independence. I would fall flat on my face plenty of times as I tripped over my own feet and sins, but I was taking steps forward.

CHAPTER 2

TRUST ME. TEST ME.

A few years ago, a friend asked me what my life verse was. At first, I didn't understand his question. He defined a life verse as a verse in the Bible that guides your decisions and challenges you to dig deeper in your faith. I knew instantly the verse that had been a guide in my life for many years, and I could pinpoint when its influence had begun.

While I continued to serve in my part-time role with the church in our hometown, Terah had found a deeper community where we attended college. I would often join her during the week for Bible studies or on special trips. In 2001, Terah and I joined the church's mission trip to Jamaica to serve in the inner city of Kingston. This would be my second mission trip and Terah's first outside of the U.S. She and I worked with a team to lead a Vacation Bible School (VBS) for nearly 400 children. During the VBS, Terah and I were always surrounded by the same little faces. For Terah, it was a little girl named Princess. For me, it was a three-year-old boy named Nicholas. Dressed every day in the same bib overalls, Nicholas would come to me in the middle of worship wanting to be held. We would dance, sing, and sweat together until he fell asleep on my shoulder. At the end of the trip, his young mother encouraged me to take Nicholas home with me to America.

I had seen poverty face-to-face plenty of times now on mission trips and in our own community, but to have a mother ask me to carry her child back to America left me stunned. I knew the immediate option was illegal, but I couldn't imagine a parent willingly sending their young child with a stranger. Sometimes, we need to be reminded of the privilege it is to live in America and to see what others see through their pair of lenses.

Toward the end of my senior year of college, as Terah and I were preparing for our wedding, the full-time children's minister position opened at the church that Terah and our friends attended. I applied for the role and was given the opportunity to serve. In a short time, more relationships developed with the kids and parents. However, within a couple of months, some of our closest friends began feeling like God was leading them to plant a church in the same area. The opportunity for Terah and I to join with our friends in church planting was extended.

The new church began in June 2002, and we were married in August 2002, after we both completed college with a degree in Elementary Education. Our first several years of marriage and church planting were filled with excitement. Terah and I were blessed in 2005 to welcome our first child, Colten, into our lives and loved being parents. We moved from our first house in the city to a large farmhouse in the country and welcomed visitors often. We started a couple of Bible study groups and held many parties for sledding, swimming, and the Fourth of July. The church began to grow as well and made an impact in the community, especially through fellowship and adult softball. We took some huge risks, and God always carried us through.

One of those risks included our lead minister joining a small group of people on a trip to Liberia, Africa. The purpose of this trip was to lead a conference on preaching and teaching; however, the God-sized purpose went much deeper. When he and the other team members returned, their hearts had been shattered for the people of Liberia, and they were deeply convicted to leverage our young church to impact the country in a big way.

Liberia was founded by freed slaves returning to Africa from the United States. The country, nearly the same in area as Tennessee, had developed into a lower middle-class society. They modeled their society from the liberties in America and consider themselves to be like a young sibling to our culture. The influences included an identical flag as ours—apart from containing only one star, not 50. Sadly, life was dramatically changed for the Liberian people throughout the course of a 14-year civil war that lasted from 1989-2003. Throughout the war, more than 250,000 lives were lost, infrastructure was decimated, and generations of farmers and skilled workers left behind an enormous group of young people under-equipped for daily life. Skills like farming returned to a trial-and-error system, while thousands faced death each year from malaria and waterborne illnesses. It would be several more years before Liberia would begin to see improvements in their population, which had dropped to 4.5 million.

It was through this time of learning about the needs in Liberia and other mission locations that God removed the hidden sin from my heart and replaced it with a heart of mission serving. As a result of my newfound passion, I attempted to publish some missionary travel lessons for children's ministry called "Truth Travelers." The idea was based on the first missionaries in the Bible—Paul, Silas, Timothy, and all who walked with Jesus. When the publishing was unsuccessful, it became a group of mission-focused children instead: a group of kids dedicated to encouraging missionaries, raising money to help hurting children in other countries, and serving the neighbors around them through prayers and service. At one point, the children were even interviewed by a Christian magazine after we dressed like starving children. We had gone door to door in a community to become more aware of the reality that millions of children experience in our world every day.

In the Spring of 2007, I had begun planning for our fifth year of Vacation Bible School. It's like a super-charged kids' church reunion complete with big activities, decorations, crafts, and many volunteers. Leading a VBS requires a lot of time and focus, and often the message seems to get lost in the details. I wanted this year to be different for the kids. I reviewed several options and landed on one called "Take the Plunge." The program centered around water with a mission focus; however, it was the main verse that connected to me the most.

Proverbs 3:5-6 (NIV) says, "Trust in the Lord with all your heart and lean not on your own understanding. In all your ways acknowledge Him and He will make your path straight."

I had probably read this verse at least a thousand times and even used it as a teaching tool; but the more I thought about it, the more something kept tugging at my heart. I wondered when the last time was that I had put my trust in God. I knew God was always there for me. He had kept me on the straight path (except the times I'd chosen differently) . . . but did I really trust Him? Did I really believe that He could do something if I stepped out in faith like the men and women in the Bible? I began to even question if He was a different God than the one who told Noah to build a boat or parted the sea for Moses. If I stepped out in faith, would He show me that I could trust Him?

One day, in my personal time of study, I read in the book of Malachi an exchange between the Lord and His chosen people, the Israelites:

> *"I the Lord do not change. So you, the descendants of Jacob, are not destroyed. Ever since the time of your ancestors you have turned away from my decrees and have not kept them. Return to me, and I will return to you," says the Lord Almighty. "But you ask, 'How are we to return?' "Will a mere mortal rob God? Yet you rob me. But you ask, 'How are we robbing you?' "In tithes and offerings. You are under a curse—your whole nation—because you are robbing me. Bring the whole tithe into the storehouse, that there may be food in my house. Test me in this," says the Lord Almighty, "and see if I will not throw open the floodgates of heaven and pour out so much blessing that there will not be room enough to store it. I will prevent pests from devouring your crops, and the vines*

in your fields will not drop their fruit before it is ripe," says the Lord Almighty. "Then all the nations will call you blessed, for yours will be a delightful land," says the Lord Almighty." —Malachi 3:6-12 (NIV)

This was it! Through the Vacation Bible School, we would test God!

I needed to see God do something that I couldn't ignore. Deep down, I knew He could answer any request, but I needed to experience his power firsthand. I really can't explain why, but the words, "Test me, Matt," just kept ringing in my heart. It was as if God was daring me with a "Bring it on" to deepen my faith in Him.

As these words kept ringing in my heart, the main verse for VBS also kept speaking to me.

"Test me . . ."

"Trust me . . ."

We had not done a missions focus for VBS, or really even tried reaching outside the church walls; so we decided to put it all together into a huge test-God moment. Instead of bigger and better stage décor, we would leverage the week to do something to serve others globally. I researched and talked to other ministry connections, and we decided on providing safe water for Liberia through water purification systems. Instead of doing more internally-focused programming, we would take the VBS to the streets and invite kids directly with a seven-foot-tall Penguin mascot.

After a little more research, I learned that each water purification system would cost around $2,000 and would give safe drinking water to an entire community. We averaged nearly 100 kids at our VBS program, and if each kid brought $80, we could reach a goal of $8,000 in one week. That was it: $8,000 from 100 kids would give four safe-water systems to the people of Liberia!

Stepping out in faith is exciting! It's like walking through a haunted house immediately after drinking an energy drink. You have no idea what's coming next, but you get so pumped up about it that you feel ready to take on the world.

I was excited to step out in faith and was not afraid to talk to anyone about it. I met with small groups of adults and challenged them to think about Liberia and many other places where two out of three people do not have access to safe drinking water. In fact, millions of people must draw water from the same water holes that animals use for bathrooms. Terah and I had been raising some ducks in our backyard, so their dirty water pool became a very effective teaching tool. I offered adults the choice to drink from either the duck water or the clean water. Thankfully, no one accepted my offer on the duck water, as we noticed that it burned holes in the small paper cups.

As the time for the VBS grew closer, the excitement was growing in the kids and even in the adults. Our outreach into the community was also producing fruit, and several kids were set to follow the penguin mascot to VBS when we began. As a team, we agreed not to do any corporate fundraising, but a fun incentive was offered: we would divide the kids into three teams, with each minister on staff representing a team. The team that raised the most money would slime the other two teams if and when we reached our goal of $8,000.

By the time the first night arrived, you could feel the energy of being part of something special. Would we break the goal of $8,000 on the first night?

When the kids entered the worship center, it appeared that this would be the case. Their arms were filled with bags and buckets of change. Some kids had given up birthday parties and asked for the money instead to help kids in Liberia. Other children had been doing special chores to earn money to give away. With huge smiles, they carried their offerings to their larger team buckets and poured in everything they had. The children had given all they had and the total on night one was $3,600!

For the next four nights, the kids continued to pour their buckets of change as an offering to God; but as Friday drew closer, it seemed the goal had been set too high. Each day as I carried a five-gallon bucket of change to the bank, I would pray for God to turn the pennies to quarters. The coins didn't change and by the time we reached Friday, our last day, we were still $3,400 short of the goal. I couldn't believe that in the evening I was going to have to stand in front of the kids and tell them that we didn't reach our goal. While I should have been grateful for the lessons of joyful giving, I couldn't imagine explaining to the kids that they had been faithful with the little things, yet God had not been faithful with the big. Wow, was my perspective off. As the day went on, I had run these thoughts through my mind constantly.

The more these thoughts consumed me, my heart began to change. What if this entire thing was about God inviting us to test Him so that we could watch Him at work? I became excited about what God might do that evening. I sent out an email to much of the church, called some friends, and invited anyone I knew to show up to church that night and watch what God was going to do.

That night, the stage was set, the buckets were in place, and the kids started arriving. I really don't know where they kept getting their money from all week, but their arms were full again with overflowing bags and buckets. As they ran toward the front with huge smiles, it was like they knew what was going to happen. They were so excited to give their gifts away to God, and their joy was contagious. We worshipped and we counted change. When the kids returned from their rotations, they only wanted to know one thing: had we reached the goal?

With tears in my eyes and an abundance of joy in my soul, I announced to the kids that we had not reached our goal—we'd broken it! God had broken it! They'd needed to bring $3,400 and instead they'd brought $3,600! The storehouses—or, at least buckets—were full and overflowing! At that point, the party had already started. We worshipped God, we danced, and every leader was slimed!

CHAPTER 3

IF GOD . . .

n Judges 6, Gideon, a little-known man from a little-known tribe, is hand-picked by God to lead Israel. He immediately replies with an "if God." An "if God" is often a promise between man and God based on God's response. After the "if God" moments of Gideon, God patiently answers each request. Gideon makes a sacrifice and God consumes it with fire. Gideon replies by being obedient to God at nighttime, when his obedience to God has the lowest risk. When God requires him to step up and lead the people into battle, Gideon responds with a couple more "if God" requests. The first request is for the fleece on the ground to be wet from dew while the ground around it remains dry. God answers early the next day, so Gideon uses another "if God": this time, the fleece must remain dry while the ground around it becomes wet with dew. God responds and Gideon obeys. Gideon leads the people into an unusual battle that includes the enemy defeating themselves and running away with fear from torches and broken jars. That day and every day after, Gideon realizes he cannot take credit for the victory, but he can always choose to be obedient.

The excitement, energy, and sacrifice of the VBS set an inspiring example for the adults. Two months after the VBS, the adults in our church were challenged to a three-year commitment of sacrificial giving centered around the story of David and Goliath. The goal would be to build a community center attached to the current church building and to give substantially to our mission partners.

From the lesson provided by the example of the kids and fueled by the new trust we had in God, we wanted to experience more of His blessings. Terah and I joined the church commitment well beyond our comfort. To stay at home with Colten, Terah put her teaching career on hold. This meant we would only live on one income. To reach this faith goal would require personal sacrifice. We started gathering things we didn't need, like my puppet collection and the Breyer model horse collection from my childhood. We held a yard sale of other items and then reset our budget to give more each month. We put our focus and trust into God. We had no idea how He would provide for this commitment or our own personal needs as He led us down an impossible road.

There is a very common statement that goes, "when it rains it pours." This statement typically is used to describe a set of tragedies or unexpected events. In our faith journey, something similar happens. When God begins to show you one thing or provides for you in a certain area, you begin to see Him provide and move in several ways.

A month after making the commitment to our church, we joined the church leadership in October 2007, on a retreat to Atlanta, Georgia, for a global leadership conference. From the first moment, we loved everything about the conference, and we felt pulled in and engaged. The speakers were challenging and inspiring, and the worship was a small glimpse of heaven. Eleven thousand church leaders from all around the world left behind their denominational differences and worshipped as one united church.

During the first main session, the speaker invited a couple to share their story about adoption. To that point, the conversation about adoption had been on the back of our minds. It had been a seed planted in Jamaica years prior with a young mother and her son, Nicholas. Terah and I listened to the couple's story about trying to pay off debt. The couple had $10,000 remaining and had settled with God that they would pursue adoption once the debt was complete. They laid out their fleece before God. Soon, another couple they didn't know met them on the sidewalk with a gift of $10,000. The couple paid off their debt and pursued adoption.

As the first session ended and we started to leave, we were handed a book, *Children of Hope: Be Touched. Be Inspired. Be Changed*, by Vernon Brewer with Noel Brewer Yeattes. That night, I sat down and started reading the stories on the pages: children in our world living in more brokenness than I could fathom. A couple of times, as I gulped back tears, I paused to tell Terah about another child's story. I had been out of the country several times, so I knew that parts of the stories had to be true, but I found myself captivated by the stories I was reading and wrestling with our personal responsibility in light of these realities.

Throughout the rest of the conference, it seemed that God had painted a bullseye on our hearts and would have won the Olympics for a repeated perfect archery score. No matter what direction we turned, the theme was constant for us: adoption. By the time we left the two-day conference, we were fully convinced.

We made it home from the conference, and our hearts continued to be burdened. We were willing to make the leap to international adoption, but we had a legitimate pause button: international adoptions are expensive and can range from $15,000–$30,000 per child including airfare and travel expenses. For a couple of months, this reality kept the idea of adoption at bay; but it felt like God just kept pushing and prodding us toward trusting Him more deeply.

For fun, I would ask Terah, "If God provided, would we adopt?" Her response was more often a "when He provides or when we get things in the right order," but we were always on the same page. Then, one day, I was driving home for a nice date night with my bride. I was listening to a Christian radio station and Tony Dungy, hall of fame coach of the Indianapolis Colts, was giving an interview about orphans and adoptions.

I turned up the radio a little bit when Tony said, "If God has called you to something, He has already provided what you need."

That night, as we were driving, I told Terah about what Tony said on the radio. Then, instead of being funny, I was a lot more serious. I asked, "We both believe God is calling us toward adoption. If God provides, will we trust Him?"

Terah replied, "If God provides, we are in."

The next day was the opening night for our children's church's Christmas musical. After the show, as the kids were heading home, one of the moms came up to me and stressed that I should not lose the envelope she was giving me for Christmas. She even asked if she needed to give it to my wife, because she was worried I would lose it. I assured her it would be fine, and she handed me the card. I finished cleaning up and went to the church sanctuary. By the time I had finished in the sanctuary, everyone else had gone home. I sat down on the pew to rest and the curiosity of the envelope in my back pocket took over. A good husband probably would have waited, but when I opened the card, read the note, and saw the gift inside, I knew that God was doing something big again. The Christmas card included a check for $3,000!

I drove home to Terah and showed her the gift. We were stunned, overwhelmed, and excited all at once. We knew immediately that the gift was not for us personally to spend on things we did not need, and we knew from research what steps we needed to take toward adoption. The next week, we called as many adoption and home study agencies as we could find. Nearly every phone call led to one response: "If you don't have at least $3,000 in the bank, then adoption isn't for you!"

Entering 2008, Terah was extremely focused on getting all of our paper-work completed to remove any delays from bringing our children home—whomever they would be. In multiple meetings, interviews, home studies, and background checks, we narrowed our criteria for adoption to up to two children under the age of two years old from Liberia, Africa.

After nearly six months of hurrying to get documents in order, we began the process of waiting—waiting to be matched; waiting to accept a child's referral; waiting on God to give us clear direction. While we waited, we applied for grants to help with adoption costs. We were denied for all of them. While we waited, we prayed for wisdom and clear directions. While we waited, we often wondered if our obedience to trust God was limited to just starting a process that we might never complete.

We made promises to God that included never giving up on our kids once we were matched together and had faces with names. We committed to joining our church's mission team to Liberia in February 2009, and began fundraising for that as well. One of the fundraisers was a huge church yard sale in which, our son, Colten, now three years old, was given a stuffed black doll to play and sleep with. It was a simple way to help his young mind understand that love comes in all skin colors.

One of the agencies that was unable to provide financial assistance sent a devotional to read and study as we continued to wait. The devotional challenged us to keep our eyes on the prize and to continue to trust God in the adoption process. It was during this time and beyond that we came to understand a few more things about the adoption process, especially in Liberia. The adoption process never makes sense and is certainly not easy, but a faith journey is rarely easy or predictable. Adopting a baby from Liberia is very unusual. The timing is never what you think it will be. The costs will always be much higher than you anticipate, and they are not always of a financial nature. God's hand at work will never be more evident than when you're in a journey such as this one.

Then one day, in mid-October 2008, after nearly a year from the time we felt God leading us down the road of adoption, we received a call from our adoption agency. A baby boy, six months old, had just come to the orphanage in Liberia with whom we were working. We discussed this baby's limited information and quickly replied with acceptance. We called all our family and friends to announce to the world we were having a boy and our son's name was Onah!

As we prayed for our precious Onah to arrive home, we also felt like God had another gift in store. Just two weeks later, we were out moving some things for a church event. I was borrowing a truck and trailer from a couple of friends when we received the next call from our adoption agency. This time, the referral was for a two-month-old girl, Marie. We were sent her information by email with a picture and instantly knew that she was meant for our family. We called our agency back to accept her referral and were suddenly struck broadside in the truck. Thankfully, everyone in the accident was okay, but the truck had been totaled. Our daughter had literally come crashing into our lives and we couldn't wait to have both children home.

With two children now at the center focus of our adoption story, there were many additional commitments, as well. The foster care fees were set at $225 per month per child, a room needed to be prepared for our children to arrive home, and new paperwork was required. Since this was a faith journey, we had started to believe that God was more than able to take care of each of these needs. We began supporting both of our kids at the cost of $450 per month. Since this would be a short commitment before they came home, we decided that a loan would be the simplest option.

The year 2008 closed quickly, and our focus was entirely on what God was going to do in 2009! Our house was being transformed to welcome two babies, and our hearts were exploding with anticipation to see God's plans work out again.

CHAPTER 4

PIGS, CANS, AND PROVISIONS

For those watching the 1992 Olympic Games in Barcelona, there was likely no more powerful story of perseverance than that of British sprinter Derek Redmond. He was doing well in the 400-meter race when his hamstring tore, dropping him immediately to the ground. He remained in his lane and struggled to his feet through pain and tears. He had already lost the race, but he was determined to finish. As he began limping down the track, his father jumped out of the stands, ran onto the track, and helped his son cross the finish line. Because of his father's assistance, Redmond was disqualified from the race, but his story continues to inspire many.

Each of our lives are often defined by how we respond to trials—when a loved one passes away, suddenly leaving a family without closure or answers; when a job ends abruptly, forcing us to seek work to provide for our families; when a family moves and their entire community is lost; or when we just can't seem to catch a break at school or home. We all face trials in our lives. Some of these trials paralyze us, while others strengthen us.

Entering into 2009, our sights were set on a mission trip, ministry, and soon bringing our kids, Onah and Marie, home from Liberia. It was going to be an exciting year for our family, and we felt ready for anything coming our way. The bedrooms for both children had been completed, and we even transitioned to becoming a van family.

While plans were finalized for our mission trip in February, we learned that our mission team would travel past our children's orphanage in Monrovia nearly every day on our way to serve others. We certainly wanted to make sure that our focus was on serving with the mission, but did not want to miss any opportunities to bring home our two waiting children. In many ways, it almost seemed like God was working out every miraculous detail to bring our kids home earlier than anticipated. We were traveling with our church family who already loved our children, our plane tickets had already been paid for—cutting the cost of adoption travel significantly—and our kids would be home before their first birthdays!

Just two weeks before the plane departed for Liberia, the first trial came crashing into our lives. Thankfully, the Government of Liberia was made aware of enormous issues around child trafficking that were believed to include nearly 400 children from Liberia to the U.S. and Canada. Due to this concern, the President of Liberia placed an immediate moratorium on all adoptions, including ours, and our case was put on hold indefinitely along with many others.

Refusing to give up hope for a miracle, we set our sights on being prepared for the impossible to happen despite the ban on adoptions. You can't pray for a miracle and doubt that God is not able, right? We boarded the plane with the team and made our way to Liberia, Africa, for the first time.

After being in the country a couple of days, we were given permission to go and see our children. With great excitement, we brought several team members with us, and quickly were ushered into the babies' room to meet our son and daughter. For Terah and I, the moment was sweet. For our children, it seemed overwhelming and terrifying, as our faces looked like nothing they had ever seen before. They were being thrust at us by the joy-filled orphanage staff. Being together was filled with moments of holding, hugging, and feeding our now ten-month-old son and six-month-old daughter.

We spent a couple of hours at the orphanage with our kids nearly every day and still maintained our focus on the mission. Together with the team, we led a community VBS for 400 children, held a very large medical clinic, joined together each night for worship, and even spent some time on the local radio station.

Multiple times, we pled with the government to allow our children to come home. As the end of our mission trip drew nearer, the chance for a miracle seemed to dim to a flicker of hope. A couple of days before we were to depart, we made our strongest connection with a government official. The response from the official was very brief, and not what we had hoped. She declared without hesitation that our children would not return with us. That meant we would have to come back for them when the ban on adoptions was lifted, and no one knew when that would be. Our final days were now filled with brokenness.

When Terah and I returned to the guest house from our last visit with our babies, we were broken. We made a quick call to our three-year-old son, Colten, to tell him that his siblings would not be coming home with us. Our faith and hope for a miracle were shattered into pieces. The tears of anticipation and frustration flowed freely. Our team members attempted to comfort us, but traveling home without our kids had not been an option. We truly did not comprehend God's plans in this process. We were thankful for the brief moments with our children as we were forced to trust again that God would work out all the details.

I spent a lot of time playing baseball as a child. I was always determined to hit a home run. One of my older brothers had hit one, so I knew it was possible. The problem for me was that I really struggled to read the different pitches. They all looked the same to me until my bat missed the ball and

I turned to walk back to the dugout with another strikeout. Life is filled with curveballs, changeups, fastballs, and sliders. It might be less about hitting the ball and more about getting back in the box to try again, each time more determined to hit the home run!

Returning home to empty beds and unworn clothes was hard for our family. The yard-sale doll Colten had been sleeping with was now tossed aside and forgotten as his young faith also took a huge hit. In that season, we disagreed with the Lord on many things. We believed His timing and methods were inaccurate and the financial cost was beyond what we could maintain for an extended period of time.

Soon after the mission trip, I was contacted about being a guest speaker the following year. I had never been asked to be a guest speaker for "big people" church, especially a year in advance, but the location was even more peculiar. The church that had released my father from full-time ministry asked me to come back and give updates about what God was doing in Liberia, Africa. I accepted the opportunity and knew that God would work in my life to remove any bitterness that had grown and replace it with forgiveness and grace.

Waiting patiently is not something I have ever mastered, and waiting on the Lord to work out details felt as if we did not want our kids home bad enough. We decided to exhaust all options in hopes that one door would open the door for our adoption to be finalized.

We sent letters to high-ranking U.S. government officials and made many phone calls to plead our case. One of those letters was sent to a senator's office prior to a special meeting that was set with the President of Liberia. We followed up on the letter with a phone call. Surprisingly, there was another Matthew Lee serving on the senator's staff at the time, so my name reference allowed me to speak with the direct and personal secretary. However, when I explained why I was calling it was made clear I was a different "Matthew Lee." The conversation was ended swiftly, and we were told the matter of adoptions would not be a part of any discussions.

With an unknown deadline to the extended time remaining in Liberia for our children, our expenses began to add up quickly. The costs that included $450 monthly foster care fees, adoption fees, and other miscellaneous expenses were beyond what we could maintain or even borrow. The reality for other waiting families led to the end of their adoption journey, while still other cases were completed despite the adoption ban. In one case, an older brother was able to come home while the younger brother remained in Liberia. As the financial pressure continued to grow, it often seemed that our dreams would not become realities and that our hope to adopt would not be possible.

Friendships surrounding us began to be fractured. Well-meaning friends challenged us to forego the rest of our adoption and felt the process had caused more hurt than it was worth. Putting our hope in God alone to guide us through, we utilized many more "if God" moments and promised God that, as long as He provided, we would stay the course, no matter the cost.

This time of waiting forced us to get more creative. We cashed in Terah's retirement plan and sold my motorcycle to cover our pledge to the church. We had several friends and family members who volunteered to join with us financially every month until our kids came home. Some friends allowed us to sell things they had around their houses, while others collected piles of metal and soda cans to be recycled. In a converted pull-behind trailer that had been made to look like Noah's traveling puppet ark, I took loads of cans and metal almost weekly to exchange for adoption funds. One couple also made special tokens to sell on our behalf, and random love gifts were given to cover partial or full months of foster care fees. While these gifts encouraged us to keep moving forward, they still were not enough to cover all the expenses.

Up to this point, we had not done a large fundraising event. We began working with some friends to put together a truly unique experience. Instead of selling t-shirts or doing a bake sale, we planned for a greased-pig wrestling contest and a car smashing with sledgehammers. The dates were set, advertisements were sent out, and one couple even covered the expense of a radio broadcast. A nearby farmer donated six piglets for the kids to chase, and a friend from our youth allowed us to borrow some full-size swine. We purchased the materials needed, including the fence for the main wrestling event, and we were ready for an incredible day in October.

When the date arrived, the weather was cold and rainy. The crowd was small, but personal friends and family joined us for a great time. Prior to the event, a couple unable to attend gave a significant gift that covered the cost, and after the event, another family also gave a gift. At the end of the day, we had cleared just over $1,000 toward adoption-related expenses, and I had acquired six piglets that I would need to find a home for now. Against Terah's better judgment, I converted a space in our detached garage and began to raise the piglets until, due to their size, we had to make a change.

Each step of the way throughout the rest of 2009 and the beginning of 2010, God faithfully provided. We stayed the course to bring our children home no matter what it might cost us personally, and we were blessed to receive partners who joined with us monthly or with one-time gifts.

CHAPTER 5

TRANSFORMATION

n Eureka Springs, Arkansas, there is a ministry called The Great Passion Play. The focus of the ministry is to allow guests an opportunity to experience life in Bible times through replicated scenes and portrayals. Inside the park's biblically-based marketplace is a potter creating a new work of art. When I was a youth, my family traveled to see this place, and the potter was the part of the experience I remembered the most. He had worked with an intense focus to create a large vase, but as he continued to mold the clay, he could see a crack unseen to the audience. In a matter of seconds, he smashed his creation into a handful of clay and began again. When he was finished with the new vase, he explained to the audience that God is our potter and we are the clay. As God molds and shapes our lives, only He can see our flaws. To become what He has planned, sometimes it is necessary to start over.

There is a general rule during the international adoption process that you plan to prevent having a biological child born around the same time as an adoptive child enters your family. Both "births" entering the family require a great amount of focus, time, energy, and an abundance of love. We had delayed getting pregnant while we waited for our children to come home, but we longed to have another biological child. We spent some time in prayer and placed the desire before God. Early in 2010, we found out that we were expecting our second biological child in late September. This unexpected gift of grace allowed us to celebrate as other things quickly unfolded in our lives.

Not seen to those closest to us was a crack in some close relationships. Terah and I remained united but struggled greatly with the length of time it was taking for our kids to come home. We believed our children should have been home by this time, but the rooms we had prepared for them remained empty. Emotionally, we were exhausted. The friends who had advised us early on to forego our adoption began to become more vocal. When we refused to heed this counsel, the crack grew larger and began to include several other areas in our relationship. Attempting to fix the fractures ourselves became impossible.

In February, we returned to our hometown for the special Sunday preaching I had been asked to do the previous year. God had indeed worked in my heart and removed any bitterness that had grown from past experiences. I am pretty sure He even deleted my original message to ensure the focus was on helping those of the greatest need in Liberia. The time with the church was precious as the youth-filled memories flooded back and old friendships were rekindled.

By the middle of March 2010, a decision was made by the church leadership to let me go from the children's ministry position. After eight years of ministry, there would be no farewell to the children and families. Plans that had been started would remain unfinished. While we would not have made this decision on our own, there was a sense of peace for Terah and me that God had bigger plans. The change in direction gave us the freedom to seek what would be best for our family, when—or if—our children would come home. Moving from the area would allow us to leave behind the reminders of unused bedrooms still waiting to be filled more than two years later.

The next few months were filled with many transitions and unique experiences. Terah did most of the preparation for moving while chasing our now-five-year-old son around and growing our little miracle in her womb. The severance I received from the church and the steady monthly partners for our adoption allowed us to stay the course. God provided in other ways as well, including the income gleaned from recycling large piles of metal in strangers' backyards. I began submitting resumes, connecting with any church interested in a children's minister, and guest preaching whenever possible.

One of the guest preaching opportunities seemed very personal for our family situation. The main idea was centered around the popular Bible verse of 2 Corinthians 5:17 (NIV): "Therefore, if anyone is in Christ, the new creation has come: The old has gone, the new is here!"

Paul, who wrote 2 Corinthians and nearly half of the New Testament, understood well what it means to be a new creation. His previous focus on silencing the Jesus movement came to a blinding end on the road to Damascus. Paul's physical body remained the same while his life mission took an eternal turn. Once a Jesus opposer, he was now a Jesus promoter. He was a new creation, tirelessly committed to knowing Christ and making Him known. Those who truly spent time getting to know Paul would understand well that he was indeed a new creation in Christ.

In creation, few examples of transformation compare to the process of a butterfly. Beginning from an egg, a tiny caterpillar hatches and begins to eat. The feeding continues until it is unable to continue growing. Within the span of one day, the caterpillar attaches to an anchor upside down, into a "J" hook, and folds around itself. When the caterpillar is completely covered, it begins an inexplicable transformation inside what's called the chrysalis. A battle of wills ensues, like a magician performing a quick-change act. A brief pause occurs, and then it happens: the new creation emerges. This creation is no longer a caterpillar but a magnificent butterfly. The wings spread, dry, and begin flapping. Finally, the adult butterfly launches out to find food.

Transformation is rarely easy or simple. It requires patience. It requires trust. It requires an understanding that we are a new creation created in Christ Jesus to do good works. We may disagree often with God's methods and His direction, but as we trust Him and walk in obedience, our story is formed for His glory.

I am not the type of person who likes to lose control of a situation, and we were living in a very uncontrolled situation at this time, which included the upcoming birth of a new baby, an unknown ending to the adoptions, and the moving of our family to an unknown location. Much like the caterpillar, I fought hard with everything in me, but the changes still came. It was only in the moments in which I gave up control that I realized God was using this season to transform our family for His glory. I didn't emerge as a beautiful butterfly, but we emerged together ready to see where God was going to take our young family, which was currently spread across two continents.

By the middle of June, after a couple of months of interviews and traveling, it was clear that God was leading our family to Lexington, Kentucky, to serve in children's ministry once again. From the first steps into this new place and often throughout the transition, God reminded us that He had prepared this area for us to serve and grow in as a family. We were warmly welcomed and encouraged to continue with our adoption. We decided that I would live with a couple of very generous families while Terah finished getting our house ready to sell in Indiana. When possible, Terah and Colten would join me on the weekends for church. Within a month, one family allowed us to move into their home entirely free for six weeks while we searched for our new home.

Together as a family again, we took the next steps of selling our Indiana home by owner and finding a small house in Lexington close to the church. We knew the house could be home for now; however, it would likely be too small when our children came home from Liberia. Our house in Indiana sold quickly and for a profit! In fact, it was more than a small profit—it was enough to pay off the adoption loan we had against the house, along with the exact amount needed to redo our home study in Kentucky for our adoption.

With our house sold in Indiana, we were able to focus entirely on getting established in Kentucky. The first step included enrolling Colten into a school that was near the church. Our church was much larger, with a lot more moving parts, and the community of Lexington was nearly five times the size of Muncie. We were blessed with some tremendous friends that took a genuine interest in the adoption process, the upcoming birth of our baby girl, and making sure we did not get lost in the area.

One day, as I was walking Colten into school, I was stopped by the guidance counselor. She explained that there were many needs inside the school, both physical and emotional, for her students, and that fewer resources and budget cuts continued to make things difficult. She wondered if our church would be interested in partnering with the public school to better serve the children. This idea had been something I had tried for years previously, but schools had not been welcoming to the idea of a church-and-school partnership. Now, we as a church were being invited in to work together.

I am thankful that, over the next several years, this partnership grew in many ways. Together, we hosted large block parties, packed hundreds of backpacks full of food and school supplies, linked tutors with kids and encouragers with teachers. It amazed me in that season that a business decided to throw away brand-new backpacks from several years of trade shows, and that God had intended these thousands of free bags to serve children in need! A church was able to help build a large memory garden, start a before-school prayer time, lead an after-school male mentorship program, and look for ways to serve with our hands and feet.

Another confirmation came in the form of an email from the children's ministry leaders in the area. I had always wanted to link with other parts of the body of Christ, but so rarely did churches desire to serve arm in arm. This group of children's ministry leaders were planning for a missionary conference. Ironically, I had been planning to bring my church kids, The

Truth Travelers from Muncie, to this same conference earlier in the year before I was released from my role at the church. By accepting the invitation, I would now be part of the planning team in Lexington!

We moved into our new home with early permission and were blessed in late September with the healthy arrival of our beautiful baby girl. Things were really falling into place in our lives; but there was still an enormous part of our hearts living in a different country. While we celebrated and praised God for the incredible gifts He had given us in the midst of very stressful times, we longed for our other two children to be home. We had already celebrated enough of their birthdays at a distance, but each time we tried to hasten their arrival, our efforts were met with complete blockades.

Thanksgiving neared, along with a scheduled commitment I'd made to a couple of Muncie kids to attend their school lunches. We decided to return to Muncie one more time. The night before Thanksgiving, we were standing in a restaurant simply catching up with some friends when my phone rang. On the other end was our adoption agency—the caller used an ecstatic tone. I stepped outside of the gathering to hear the agency director clearly say that something had happened with our children's cases. Despite the moratorium remaining in place, our documents had been approved. Our paperwork had been signed prior to the moratorium in 2008 and, for some reason, had not been located until now! Now, the only thing standing in front of our kids coming home was us finalizing our paperwork from the move to Kentucky. Surrounded by friends that had traveled this journey with us, we cried many happy tears.

We returned home after Thanksgiving determined to complete our paperwork. We would soon learn that this was not the only obstacle remaining in our path, but we were ready to face new challenges with great resolve, knowing that our kids could finally come home!

CHAPTER 6

FINALEE HOME

This is not really a book of advice, but I would like to give you some. This is not really a book about great wisdom, but experience is a great teacher. So, let me give you some advice and share with you some wisdom that I have learned from personal experience.

If you don't want your life to be radically changed—even though it will be much better than your plans—do not write God a to-do list!

Our family had begun to settle into our new normal as we anticipated the arrival of our two children coming home from Liberia—an event that could happen anytime. We were in the midst of transitioning from a family with one five-year-old to a family with four children. Each day was another day of anticipation of our updated documents being received and processed in Liberia. We were told in February 2011 that we should begin booking plane tickets and lodging, as we would get the notification at any time. We proceeded forward with plans for mid-March, giving ourselves plenty of time for delays in Liberia.

As the travel date drew closer, we received another call. In preparation for processing our children's documents, the government of Liberia conducted interviews with our children's birth mothers. Unfortunately, neither of the biological mothers were able to answer basic questions about our son and daughter's births and life details. Since the interviewers could not confirm that the mothers being interviewed were the true biological mothers, the government would require a DNA test to be completed. The delay was not expected to take more than a month or two, and the cost would be around $500 for the tests to be processed.

I was at the church office when I received the call. I called Terah to let her know, then I shared the news with two other people. The first person was a co-worker. I walked into his office, told him the frustrating news, and said to him, "I have seen God do some incredible things in this journey, and I just need Him to show up again." Then, I called my mom. I explained to her the delay and her response was nothing short of God showing up. She shared in the frustration, and then she said, "Well, your dad did a funeral of an elderly friend two weeks ago. The lady's surviving husband brought your dad an additional check after he sold a load of beans. He wanted to help with adoption expenses. The amount he brought was $500."

When I was in youth ministry, we would take a group of youth to an annual retreat. For several years, this event had hosted the same artist: his specialty seemed to be painting with a broom on a very large canvas. Music would play as he made random swipes and changed colors. The more he painted, the more confusing his painting would be. Then, when he was satisfied with his work, he would put away his broom and step back. The audience would sit stunned that this mess was a special work of art until he walked back over to the painting. Removing it from the stand, he would flip it over and reveal an incredible work of art. After one of the events, I told the artist about our adoption, and he gave me a copy of one of his works on a canvas.

While we certainly were not excited about an extra delay, this journey was all about trusting God. If God wanted to include a grieving widower in His story to bring two children home from Liberia—which seemed like an odd splash of paint—we would need to trust Him. The reality is that God was our artist, and we were simply the canvas. He alone knew what our life painting was going to look like.

A couple of months later, the tests confirmed that both mothers were indeed the biological parents, and we were given the green light to bring our kids home. As we looked at optional dates between the end of school and a very busy summer schedule in ministry, we set our dates for the end of May. This would allow us to return five days before our first Vacation Bible School in Lexington. You never know what a trip to Liberia for adoptions will require or what could happen, so we made sure the team was in place in case we missed the VBS.

The morning after we arrived in Liberia, we met our children and the Orphanage Director at the hospital to complete medical exams and make sure the kids were okay to travel. We had sent many videos to our children, along with some picture books of our family, but they were still really young. The reunion was sweet, but in many ways, it was like meeting our now three-year-old son and two-year-old daughter for the first time. The wait was long at the hospital, filled with new memories, and eventually, both children were given the all-clear.

The following days were filled with meetings and interviews with the embassy and the Ministry of Gender staff. We spent some free time working on projects at the orphanage and making fun memories in Liberia together. Each day was a new adventure for us all, including passport photos, collecting required signatures, ice cream, Sprite, and pizza. We spent several moments at the nearby beach and a lot of time in our guest room just bonding together. We enjoyed moments of utilizing technology to have our kids in America talking to our kids in Liberia. They were all excited to meet each other, and we could not wait to have our family all together under one roof on the same continent.

At the end of one very busy day that had included our son pulling a TV over on himself and a trip to a less-than-equipped ER, our little family in

The Lee family. (I am in the middle.)

Terah and I riding Chance. (He is mentioned at the beginning and end of the book.)

Onah and Marie coming home June 9, 2011. (The family is now all together in one country.)

The vision was born based on this dinner tray. A secure wall surrounding a boys' foster home, girls' foster home, medical clinic, church, school, and administration building.

The orphanage remodel team. (November 2012)

The 2014 team. (We traveled during Ebola and began Psalm 82:3 Mission.)

Colten's first mission trip. (June 2016)

The Crump family uniting with their children Jeff and Mahari. (June 2016)

The vision team. (September 2017)

The ladies from the AFAA home growing up together in Lexington, Kentucky.

The Fann family returning home with their daughter Quita in 2018. Quita is Blessing's best friend from the orphanage.

Terah and I meeting Onah and Marie for the first time in February 2009.

Tamme and her children serving in Liberia. My brother Bill is the tallest guy in the middle.

Liberia was exhausted. Each day, I attempted to journal our experiences so we could look back on them and see God's hand of faithfulness. Not able to journal in a dark hotel room, I went outside to our balcony area. The night is often louder than the day because the sounds that fill it include generators powering hotels, businesses, and homes for those that can afford them. I sat for a few minutes to recall the adventures and challenges of the day, and how unique those moments would have been to us in America. As I wrote, however, my pen, heart, and mind were constantly reflecting on the faces and conditions of the orphanage home.

Despite the reality that they had no true play area, the fifteen children still laughed and played like every other child. Unfortunately, the ban on adoptions that still existed had taken a significant toll on the physical structure of the orphanage home. The staff was doing their best to get through each day. Each time I visited, I would be asked to look at different projects in hopes that I could make some improvements. A few of those projects included a leaking roof that had led to water falling on sleeping children, burst septic pipes that made the play area a wasteland, and the main electrical wiring being bound together by trash bags. To be honest, I was frustrated that God did not know this was the condition of the home for His children in Liberia; yet every day and every night, they worshipped Him. With this in mind, I wrote:

If the kids are going to be in an orphanage, they should be in a great orphanage.

Buy the building/house—it is solid structurally, but it does need a lot of work! Stop renting!

MISSION TEAM
Replace wiring and lights in all rooms (include ceiling fans)
Replace roof with potential solar panels
Repair septic drains/install clean water system
Replace entrance by digging out driveway
Build a library with shelves and computers—finish a secure place for the orphanage director to work!

Paint all rooms (boys like boys & girls like girls & babies like babies)
Get sponsors for all kids remaining
Build a playground
Tons of clothes, shoes, sandals, etc.
Two nice, easy-to-drive cars
Put stone/gravel in road

I wrote out a budget breakdown for staff salaries, rent, repairs, education, clothing, and medical, and I even created a plan for God to get the funds for the projects.

Child sponsors get letters, pics, and updates.
All sponsors get general updates from orphanage.

I vow to put this to rest until God opens the doors! The sign is ten people asking what they can do to help the other kids!

With this now off of my mind, I felt I had really been a huge help to God. I had delivered to Him a list to follow in hopes that He would improve the conditions of the orphanage. My mind was at peace.

The phrase "armchair quarterback" is used to describe a person who does not participate in the action but still makes judgements about it. We yell at the TV when our favorite team is playing, and it's obvious from where we're sitting what the best plays are. It's weird that we do the same thing with God.

Despite a few challenges with the Liberian government—employees not showing up for work for a couple of days, and delays in our flights—the rest of the trip went smoothly. On January 8th, we began our journey home with our two children whom we had waited nearly three-and-a-half years to have home. Soon, they would meet their two siblings, whom they had heard so much about, face to face. The flights home went well, with the exception of a small delay from Atlanta to Lexington. By the end of the day, we walked our son and daughter down the steps toward baggage claim, where they were greeted by their older brother, baby sister, family, and several friends. It was a beautiful moment together and included more pictures than we could count.

On the drive home, we began a new tradition of getting McDonald's for dinner to celebrate our family being together and our children's homecoming day. We had originally planned for special moments of giving God thanks, but the journey home had removed all remaining energy from our bodies. It was time for one of the best nights of rest we had ever had—our family was all together, and we were finally home!

The following days, weeks, and even months quickly became a blur as we adjusted to family life and ministry life in the midst of a very busy summer. A few days after arriving home, our kids were surrounded by many new faces at church, VBS, and church camp. We were greatly loved during those next few weeks and began to make friends with people who would one day become family through our connection at the nearby church camp. Our small group was an enormous blessing as well, giving us the space we needed to adjust but taking an enormous interest in the current conditions of the orphanage in Liberia. I often would reflect on the list I had given God and wonder who He would lead to do something about the situation. As I reflected, I was reminded of God's faithfulness to us as we made memories together on our farm, at local fairs, and just being together as a family.

CHAPTER 7

ICE CREAM SUNDAE

n 2012, Matthew West wrote a song called, "Do Something." The premise of the song centers around the times we do not like what we see in our world and, instead of acting, we expect God to fix it for us. We expect God to fix homelessness, human trafficking, broken marriages, and addictions that destroy our lives. As we are "shaking our fist at God," asking Him to do something, it might be that He simply replies to us, "I did. I created you!"

Jesus was asked by a teacher of the law—who hoped to trip up the Master—what the most important commandment was. In Matthew 22:37-40 (NIV), Jesus gives a simple reply.

> *"Love the Lord your God with all your heart and with all your soul and with all your mind. This is the first and greatest commandment. The second one is like it: Love your neighbor like you love yourself. All the law and the prophets hang on these two commandments."*

In 2011, while preparing to bring our kids home from Liberia, my heart had been stirred about the condition of the orphanage my children called home for most of their very young lives. To be honest, I was frustrated. How could God call Himself the Defender of the Fatherless and not know that orphans around the world lived in conditions like this, or worse? Sitting on a hotel balcony in Liberia, I basically shook my fist at heaven and then wrote God a to-do list. I handed the problem and the solution over to Him and figured He could find someone qualified to take care of the need.

When we returned home after our three-and-a-half-year adoption journey, we were tired. I felt like we had done what God had wanted us to do in trusting Him to adopt two beautiful children. Emotionally and financially, we were spent. We were trying to focus on bonding our young family. From chance encounters to small groups and new church camp friends, our conversations always came back to the condition of the orphanage. Secretly, I was praying that one of these people who kept asking questions would be the person to lead the team. I had worked in construction for a couple of years during college breaks, but I didn't really see myself as the person to lead a team of contractors. However, nearly every listener said that they would support or go if I would lead.

After several months of trying to push this task onto someone else, the Matthew West song started playing on the radio. I listened to it several times before realizing this song just might have been written for me. I decided that, if I was going to lead the team, I was taking the best contractors this side of the Atlantic Ocean. I put together an application and reached out to every professional builder, electrician, and plumber I could think of. Then, I waited. To my shock, not one of them replied with interest or even a desire to travel to Liberia. I did receive interest from unlikely, but very willing, people—a friend from high school in the middle of a career change; a successful funeral director; and a world-renowned entomologist and photographer.

After a couple of months, we had added a few more team members. We waited for at least one person to be a professional contractor. Just eight days before our flight, one team member joined who was at least familiar with building in conditions like Liberia. At the time of departure, fifteen people were on the team. The stories behind each of them joining us were nothing short of God at work.

There were many other details God worked out as well. The financial need was $5,000 for all projects, yet we were equipped with more than $10,000. A local store had provided all of our equipment at cost or donated high quality tools. A school system gave us special-needs equipment for free to serve the children with disabilities at the orphanage. When our team departed the Lexington airport, the gentleman who loaded our luggage was from Liberia. All luggage, plus a generator, arrived when the team arrived. On top of that, all team members traveling from across the country also arrived on time and safely to Liberia.

Nehemiah is a great book in the Bible that seems to be often overlooked. He was a cupbearer in another land who accepted the challenge to rebuild the city walls in his home country. He led the people to do something they had not been able to accomplish on their own. His method was simple: challenge people to build the area that impacted them the most. If the wall was broken down in front of your house or business, it was of great interest to you to secure that location. Nearly everyone in the community helped, and in fifty-two days, the wall of Jerusalem was rebuilt. Throughout his story, Nehemiah's testimony outlines clear steps to being an effective leader. It was from the lessons of Nehemiah that the mission team was organized.

Upon arrival in Liberia, we drove to the orphanage, where we would stay. We did not want to waste time or money on hotels and extra travel. We only had four business days to get the work done and wanted to be as wise as we could with the time. The first morning, we were awakened by a room full of grateful kids, but not for us. They were grateful to God for His provision. They greeted God each morning and night with praise and worship. That was all the motivation the team needed. We divided ourselves into focus groups with a list of projects, and hired Liberian workers at ten dollars per day to work alongside of us.

Team 1: Build a playground (a special project funded and planned by a graduating high school senior who had been adopted from Liberia)

Team 2: Redo all electrical (led by a doctor who learned to wire a house during the plane ride)

Team 3: Paint house, paint fence, repair broken window screens, and repair kitchen

Team 4: Plumbing and repair septic infrastructure

Team 5: Paid contractors for tearing off and putting on a new roof

The first day, the team worked hard and seemed to not tire. If they did get tired, they would look over at one of the kids in the orphanage or stop working long enough to play with one of them. Then, it was back to work. I knew that our time was limited, but sleeping on kid-sized beds, changes in diet, and limited rest options formed my main concern: that a team member might get sick or too worn out. At the end of the first workday, I turned off the generator at 5 p.m. A few seconds later, the generator was turned back on—not by me, but by a team member. This team member explained that our time was short and we had a purpose. He also declared that we would rest when we could not work any longer.

For the rest of the days, that was exactly what the team did. During the entire trip, a team that had mostly met in Liberia never squabbled, whined, or weakened. They were united and determined, and each person owned their roles perfectly. By the end of four working days, we had completed over thirty projects of all sizes! The roof was replaced, the electrical work was completed safely, the septic systems repaired, the playground built, and much more. Since we were in Liberia with extra funds, we gave approval for other projects to be completed after we departed. One of those projects was to move the main entrance gate to a different side of the orphanage space to allow vehicles to enter. On our last day, they had already removed the old gate and knocked down the wall where the new gate would be installed.

Departing the orphanage at the end of our week was an experience filled with a variety of emotions. There was celebration from witnessing what God had done through this team. There was a peace from accomplishing what we had set out to do. There was hope that the orphanage was now in good shape and that we had really been able to make a difference. There was also sorrow. While we had focused on the projects, we had each connected to different kids during our time at the orphanage. As we packed up and began to depart, one of the little boys came to me. I gave him a hug and then he looked at me with tears streaming down his face.

He said, "Uncle Matt (in Liberia you quickly become family), please find me a family."

Together, through tears, we knelt together and prayed for that to happen. I knew it was not an option with the ban still in place on adoptions in Liberia, but with God, all things are indeed possible.

After leaving the orphanage and doing some shopping downtown, we arrived at our departure gate at 5:05 p.m. We were shocked to find the ticketing station closed for the day despite our flight leaving after 8 p.m. Through several strong discussions and a lot of frustration with the remaining airline workers, we learned that we would only be able to change our flights to the following day. After making the necessary changes to our flights, we prayed, cried, and watched our plane depart the country without us. An identical flight leaving the following day was extremely rare, and in our frustration, we were unable to see that God was already at work.

As far back as blueprints and topographical maps exist, there also exists a phrase: "the birds-eye view." It simply means to have an elevated perspective of an object or situation. In our faith journey, God alone has the best birds-eye view, as He can see the entire picture surrounding us. He can see the problems coming long before we can and can provide directions to avoid missteps. From our limited perspective, this is very difficult as we cannot always see what is happening around us. In those moments, we are forced to trust God's perspective.

Extremely exhausted, most of the team went in search of a hotel. All the hotels were booked for the night except one owned by a Chinese family. We negotiated for a one-night stay at $115 per room. One team member decided he wanted to make sure the kids were safe, since we had just begun working on the new entrance, so he and I returned to the orphanage to sleep.

The next day, we returned to the hotel to find that the team was rested, but other frustrations had arisen. The owner of the hotel informed us that our credit cards would not work and that we had misheard the price of the room. The price was now $150 per room for the night. As frustrations continued to mount, the owner glanced over at a team member. Using his index finger from each hand, he made the shape of the cross and asked if we were Christians. We had already explained this to him the night before, but we nodded in agreement again. Then, he looked at us and said, "You missionaries doing God's work. You stay for free."

He then asked our team to follow him upstairs as he had something he wanted to share with us. Since he had graciously agreed to let us stay for free, we agreed. We followed him and his family upstairs to a small room and he closed and locked the door.

He shared that his father had brought the family to Liberia a few years back. The majority of the family had surrendered their lives to Christ, but their father refused. In 2011, his father had been murdered on the front steps of the hotel. There was no investigation into his murder, and his family was left trying to make the business in a foreign country work. They had been praying since his passing for God to give them a sign that things were going to work out, but they had not heard anything from God. Discouraged, they stopped praying. A couple of weeks prior to our arrival they felt convicted to pray again for a sign. Then, a team of Christian missionaries walked into their hotel needing a place to stay for the night. Our team was their sign that God would work out the details! The only thing they requested from us was prayer. Together we prayed and worshipped together in multiple languages to the only One who can write stories like this.

Promptly after our time of prayer and worship, we departed the hotel for the airport. While God had certainly been at work, we did not want to take the risk of missing another flight.

Returning home, our team began to share the story from the perspective of an ice cream sundae. We had craved ice cream all week during the mission trip and at the end of the work we splurged on two gallons of melted ice cream for forty U.S. dollars. The encounter at the hotel was our cherry on top. Over the next few months, we shared with as many different groups as we could about what God had done. To our surprise, nearly every visit or conversation was followed with, "What's next?"

CHAPTER 8

CHOOSING TO DEFEND

Every life journey has at least one defining moment. Defining moments can be viewed as a fork or "T" in the road. Throughout the Bible are a variety of defining moments.

Shepherd Moses meeting with a talking bush.

Elderly Noah requested by God to build a boat.

Dreamer Joseph being tossed into a pit and sold by his brothers.

Beautiful Queen Esther visiting the king without prior permission.

The journey to adopt two children had included several defining moments. Some of the moments, choices had been easy to make, while other moments had presented difficulties. Our family had relocated, and our children had come home. The remodeling project had been completed, and stories were being told about God's provision. As these stories were being shared, more people continued to ask what was next. I was starting to feel a very real responsibility to the kids in Liberia, while also desiring to focus on my family and ministry in America. It was like my heart was in a constant state of living in two worlds.

We decided to take another team back to Liberia for a couple of weeks at the end of the summer in 2014. The goal of this trip was to serve the children with special needs and help the organization in charge of the orphanage to acquire ongoing sponsors. The team would take lots of pictures and learn each child's story well. This time, the team quickly grew to fifteen people.

As preparations were being made, a disease began to spread across Liberia and other African countries like a wildfire. The very deadly Ebola virus had claimed many lives quickly. Areas of Liberia were being closed and most people became afraid of going to a doctor for any kind of treatment. In fear, the people remained home, and the virus continued to spread. We watched closely and prayed fervently for the orphanage to be protected. We debated the wisdom of traveling to Liberia during the virus and challenged team members to pray for guidance.

In team discussions, we were reminded of a past connection to safe water systems (remember the VBS moment with the kids from earlier). The systems that delivered safe water also created a highly-potent bleach that could be very useful in protecting from the virus. When the deadline arrived to make an official decision, most of the team felt as if we had no choice. We had to deliver these safe water systems regardless of the conditions of the country.

In the classic movie, "Indiana Jones and the Last Crusade," the main character has a death-defying moment. It is believed in the movie that a drink from the Holy Grail can save his father's life. Indy makes it through several traps and reaches the edge of a cliff. There is no bridge that he can see as he lifts one foot into the air and leans forward. To his amazement, his foot lands on a bridge that leads him safely to the Holy Grail. It is nearly impossible to see where faith steps will lead, the impact they will have, or the risks involved with them.

From the very first morning in Liberia, the focus of the team was like that of the remodeling team. The team was awakened by kids worshipping and it set the tone for the rest of the trip. All projects were completed, and one water system was installed at the orphanage. We even had time for fun activities like a paint war and photo sessions with each child.

The farewell was more difficult on this mission trip. We now had a much more personal connection to the kids and staff at the home. Another two years had passed for the children who were more like our nieces and nephews, and they hadn't found their forever families. The ban on adoptions that had begun in 2009 was still in place. My little buddy from the first trip came to me again as I was packing up. He came to me weeping as I was standing next to the bed on which he had written his name. I grabbed him, and we wept together. We knelt together and prayed again for a forever family.

While waiting for our flight home from Newark, I checked emails and phone calls from the past week. One of the emails was from the organization that ran the orphanage. The note was requesting us to consider taking over the funding of the orphanage. I shared the message with the team, and what happened next was something I did not expect. The team that had faithfully journeyed to Liberia during the Ebola crisis was now deeply committed to the wellbeing of the children. As we started talking about specific roles, it became clear that God had already built a team. It was decided that I would remain in the role of storytelling and connecting to new partners. Other team members agreed to build a website, track finances, keep notes, and take over social media. We would all serve as volunteers so that every dollar given would go to help the children.

A few days after returning home, a flurry of events took place. One of the couples from the team gave an update to their Sunday School class. The church gave $2,000 in a one-time gift. This was a clear indication that we should continue moving forward. While this was happening, the reality of our proximity to the Ebola crisis and an allergic reaction to malaria medicines forced two of our team members into the hospital for several days. Another team member was appointed as a funeral expert of Ebola in case the disease made its way to Kentucky. Lastly, within a week of our return, the Government of Liberia closed all borders. Our little friends at the orphanage remained at the top of our prayer list.

The Old and New Testaments are filled with examples of God's heart for the orphans. Several times, the prophets and teachers challenged the people of Israel to take up the cause of the orphan and widow. When they chose not to obey, God's judgment was clear. When they obeyed, God's protection and provision were evident. God alone is the defender of the fatherless, and we are His physical representation. As we studied through hundreds of verses, it seemed that God's mission for our team connected best to Psalm 82:3.

Psalm 82:3 (NIV) says, "Defend the weak and fatherless, uphold the cause of the poor and the oppressed."

With the name of Psalm 82:3 Mission, we began taking more steps in faith. The more steps we took, the more we saw God move. The movement was not always in the way of major mountains, but often in the simplest molehills. Through other established ministries, we learned how to create a board of directors and organize monthly meetings. We connected to willing lawyers and worked through the many steps of complying with governmental requirements. Each step was challenging, but at the same time rewarding.

Our team worked with the orphanage director in Liberia to set a monthly budget. We added a couple staff positions and planned for basic needs, medical care, and physical therapy for the children with special needs. The costs added together for a monthly budget of $4,500.

Somehow, God always provided as His children in the United States gave generously to serve His children in Liberia. Small groups of people joined monthly or gave one-time gifts. Churches of all sizes gave generously. Our friends at Church Camp leveraged weeks of Day Camp, and a few churches used VBS programs as special collection moments. While all of these gifts and support were needed, the biggest support came from individuals choosing a child to support and connect to personally. Individuals joining monthly allowed our ministry to have a consistent amount of funding amounting to $2,800 per month.

For the next two years, God just did what He does as we trusted in Him for provision. Each month, we would pray over our deficit between the $4,500 going out and the $2,800 consistently coming in. Unable to remove anything from the budget, we witnessed as God not only provided but surpassed the need.

God has always been the Story-weaver. He alone wove Moses' mother into the kingdom that desired to kill her child. He alone led a dreamer from a pit to the palace to save his people. He alone placed peoples and groups into this story that we would never have been able to put together.

From past church connections to new friendships, we experienced story after story of God weaving together His children for His purpose. Partnerships that developed with churches, especially in the Indiana area, reconnected my family with many churches from our youth. One of our monthly sponsors became very connected to my buddy and his sibling. The deepening of the relationship between sponsor and children could only be described by the family as "divine."

Things progressed forward for Psalm 82:3 Mission, and we continued to pray for the moratorium on adoptions. Then one day, in June 2015, without any warning from the Liberian government, the ban on adoptions was lifted. That meant that our little friends at the orphanage could be matched with forever families! The first family that was matched was our dear friends from Lexington, who had connected as sponsors to our now "nephew" and "niece" in Liberia. The next step for them was paperwork and waiting.

In the waiting, we continued to serve the kids and staff monthly as well as plan for our next trip in June 2016. No matter when a trip is planned, the time between planning and traveling closes rapidly thanks to the many details to be worked out. For this team, the focus would be on installing solar power at the orphanage, which was a project amounting to nearly $24,000, and working on several other projects that had come up since our last trip in 2014. In only a month, God provided the funds for the solar project—a couple of months later, a team was sent to be trained on the solar install.

On the personal side, my oldest son (who was eleven years old) decided he wanted to join the team. To join, he would have to raise his own funds. Witnessing God provide for such a young person was incredible. He made and sold more than 250 sock snowmen right before Christmas and collected over $1,000 of his needed $3,000. The rest came from support letters and very generous donors. Along with him on the team was one of his childhood friends, our friends who were planning to adopt, several board members, and past team members who just had to be with the kids in Liberia again.

We had an incredible trip. The solar power was installed and our team led a VBS for 400 very energetic kids at an orphanage. We had lots of fun making memories with incredible kids—paint wars, photo sessions, and beach parties. In my heart and mind, though, there were two things that stood out above the rest. The first was watching my son jump out of bed every morning to serve at least eight hours each day with a little boy who was blind. He simply loved, giggled, and loved some more. The second was this incredible moment to sit down with my nephew and niece, (unofficially official) to explain adoption and introduce them to their forever parents. Glued to the window and surrounding the home were the eyes of every team member witnessing a miracle in action.

This time, leaving the orphanage was still hard. We did not know the end of the adoption story, how adoptions would impact the ministry, or what God was going to do next. We knew He was going to work out the details, but the way He continued to write this story was nothing like we would have predicted when we became defenders of the fatherless.

CHAPTER 9

HOLD ON TIGHT

The high speeds and dangerous flips of a roller coaster require the rider to buckle in tightly. The ride begins peacefully with a climb to the top, while every clink builds anticipation. Adrenaline fills the veins. The first turn comes into view, and every rider knows that soon they will be moved in both uncontrollable and exhilarating ways. It's too late to jump out. Hold on tight and enjoy the ride.

The story of Psalm 82:3 Mission has experienced many twists and turns since 2007. God guided a young couple through a three-and-a-half-year journey of adoption that included an adoption ban, broken relationships, new ministry opportunities, a baby of grace, and two children finally coming home. Before the ride ended, a list was written to God, and a new climb began. A team traveled and remodeled the orphanage, and two years later, another team traveled during the Ebola crisis. Psalm 82:3 Mission was born to fund the orphanage. Child sponsors, past church connections, and a new ministry partner allowed the ministry of volunteers to find its rhythm helping kids they knew well for more than two years. Adoptions reopened in Liberia, and our "niece and nephew" came home to Lexington, Kentucky. A couple weeks later, these children and our children, all from the same home in Liberia, were playing together while their parents led the children's area at the annual mission conference—the same conference we had connected to in 2010 when moving to Lexington.

Beginning in October 2016, we celebrated and witnessed kids being connected to their forever families. In every situation, we wished we could be a fly on the wall as each child or sibling group arrived home. The more children came home or were matched with forever families, the clearer it became that the orphanage was being mostly funded through the beauty of adoptions. By March 2017, we knew that God had brought us to the end of our partnership with the orphanage in Monrovia. Being reminded that He alone is the true defender of the fatherless, we had to trust Him to care for the children and staff we loved. We reached out to the founder and shared our decision to pay the rent, therapy for the children with special needs, and a few other things through the end of 2017.

Ending the partnership was filled with mixed emotions and curiosity. We knew we needed to move forward, but we didn't know what we were moving toward. For the first couple of monthly meetings, our team sat in a room with nothing much to say to one another. So we prayed. We began to pray fervently that God would either make it clear that we had reached the end or prepare us quickly for the journey ahead. We contacted our partners to let them know about our decision and gave them the option to end their support. To our amazement, most of our partners wanted to see what was next and continued their ongoing contributions.

In between hurriedly getting to your seat on a plane and the long flight ahead, there is a pause. Once a plane is loaded and fueled, the pilot will taxi the plane slowly around the tarmac. Reaching the runway, a final check is done, and the pilot awaits clearance from the tower. Inside, the passenger anticipation builds for takeoff. As our pilot, God knows the power of the pause in each of our lives as well. It is often in the pause that our attention turns from our plans to His.

Throughout our time of praying, we began to receive new friend requests on social media. One of those new friends, a missionary serving in Liberia, connected us to a Liberian pastor. The pastor invited us to see the possibilities in Grand Bassa County, a county we had never traveled to in Liberia. Buchanan, the main city in Grand Bassa County, is the third largest city in Liberia, with nearly 35,000 people who call it home. The county of Grand Bassa is home to nearly 250,000 people.

The invitation was simple. "If you want to help orphans and hurting kids, then you must come to Buchanan."

Before we closed the door to Psalm 82:3 Mission, it seemed wise to at least accept the invitation to visit the Buchanan area. A team of four made plans for September 2017. Not knowing the missionary or the pastor in Grand Bassa County well, we invited the assistant director of the orphanage in Monrovia to help guide us forward on the Liberian side. A couple weeks from traveling, it seemed God was already putting options into motion. We had a couple of options in front of us.

Option 1: Partnering with the U.S. missionary to revive the dream of a Christian College that was under construction before the Civil War in Liberia.

Option 2: A landowner near Buchanan desired to sell fifty acres, located on the highway, to only our ministry for the cost of $30,000.

The team arrived safely and connected to our friend from the orphanage. Leaving the airport, instead of turning to the familiar left direction of Monrovia, we turned right. This took us through the Firestone Plantation, which was filled with rubber trees and several smaller communities. An hour later, we entered the simple little city of Buchanan, Liberia. Immediately, we could sense that the pace was much slower, and the people were more friendly.

Our first connection in Buchanan was the pastor and his wife, who graciously had our team in their home every day to eat and learn. We spent many hours talking with them about their efforts to faithfully start a church and school in the local community. We joined them for church and were humbled with the deep love for Jesus and the joy in their worship. Our friends, who had survived a fourteen-year civil war and faced death from every angle, danced and sang with freedom from the soles of their feet to the tips of their fingers as they proclaimed that they were crazy for Jesus.

Beyond the conversations and church, they invited us to join their live radio Bible study and set up a three-day revival service near the main fishing docks. Toward the end of our trip, we had the honor to baptize eight individuals in the ocean. This experience was more like a WWE wrestling battle though, as our bodies were often struck by waves. To prevent being knocked down, we would quickly lift the person up, plunge them into the water, and then bring them back up by tossing them toward the beach.

The mayor of the city was our next connection—she opened her schedule to brainstorm ideas with us. When we shared our hope of starting an orphanage in Buchanan, she was very supportive but made three simple requests.

1) The orphanage must be Christian.
2) We must agree to set the example for other orphanage homes.
3) She requested that we locate our home outside the city limits, since the needs were far greater in the county.

Each day on our journey, we saw and experienced the many different faces of life in Buchanan and Grand Bassa County. We visited and served food and toys to two orphanage homes that were far worse than the home in Monrovia prior to the remodel in 2012. We visited an "old folks' home," where the conditions can't even be described. Throughout the city, children as young as three years old sold trash bags to be able to eat. It seemed that every corner held another face of desperation. Despite the needs, each person was incredibly gracious, joyful, and loving.

We spent a considerable amount of time looking at and discussing the two options that had been opened to us. Reviving the Christian College would entail several challenges. While the space would be adequate for an orphanage, we would have to rebuild most of the structures, make the current squatters homeless, and work through lengthy steps to purchase the land. The land would be safe for children, as it was far from the main roads, but the roads in rainy season might also become unpassable at times. Together, the team decided that this option would not be the wisest direction forward.

Next, we traveled to the fifty acres that were an option for purchase. This land was located on the main highway, ten miles outside Buchanan and closer to the airport. It was nearly all dense-forest area and difficult to see the potential in as we hacked with machetes for forty-five minutes to a small, open field. We had a hand-drawn map showing us the boundary lines, but seeing the entire property was nearly impossible. To have the opportunity to buy land directly on the highway provided plenty of options for growth and development, and the density of the forest had proven that the land was a good option for agriculture. The purchase of this land could be a clean slate not yet dreamed. We decided to invest in this possibility by having a path cleared around the entire fifty acres. To clear the path would take several men nearly three days, so our team took the time to return to Monrovia.

Returning to the familiar city of Monrovia would provide our team with moments outside the situation to seek God for more clarity, visit our friends at our recently-ended orphanage partnership, and meet with another pastor who had become a great advisor. The journey to Monrovia added to the experience as a tire blew out. Thankfully, a man who was mute led his village to action, a little boy sat on a stump and prayed, and one of our staff from the orphanage passed us on her way back to Monrovia. A couple of hours later, we were back on the road.

Arriving at the orphanage was much like arriving home to a family reunion. As we honked the horn announcing our arrival, everyone—including staff and kids—came to greet and hug us. While the greetings were filled with love, this arrival was not what we had expected. There was a great amount of love in the air, but the staff and kids had been made aware of our ending partnership. Along with the joy of seeing one another came moments of great sadness. For a new door to open, the door filled with love, closeness, and comfort would have to close. We only stayed with our friends at the orphanage for a couple hours before we went to our hotel for the night.

Attached to the hotel was a small diner where we could meet and discuss all the things on our hearts so far from this trip. We discussed the realities and the opportunities we had in front of us in Grand Bassa County. We laughed about our journey to Monrovia. We unpacked the emotional visit to the orphanage home. God was clearly stirring in our hearts as we placed every possibility on the table.

As we talked and prayed, our focus began to take a sharp turn. Psalm 82:3 Mission had begun in response to meeting basic needs. We often viewed our role as doing something for God and would seek God's guidance for what He wanted us to do next. As we prayed through the development of the land, our prayer and understanding changed. Instead of being about what we would do for God, it became clear that God was going to do something in Buchanan, and we could be a part of it.

In seventh grade, I was cut from the basketball team. Being cut carried a sting with it, but I knew the story of Michael Jordan. He had also been cut from his team as a youth and went on to become the greatest player to play the game. Every day after school—even through the snow—I practiced. During my practices, I dreamed of being called up to the NBA to play on the same court as the Chicago Bulls. I barely made the eighth-grade team the next year, and after my freshmen year of basketball, I announced my retirement. Nearly every young athlete dreams of being part of a great team, but the reality for Christians is that we are already part of the best team on the planet.

The next morning, we sat down as a team at the breakfast table. With the change in our hearts and prayers, ideas and dreams began to take shape. In the middle of the table was a rectangular plastic tray. The pattern on the tray caught our attention: there were several squares around the outside edge with lines attaching to each square. In the middle was a large blank space. Each square in our minds represented a building, and the line was a block security wall. We identified several of the squares: orphanage homes, an administration building, a medical and therapy clinic, a home for babies and medically-fragile children, a church, a school, and even a home for the elderly. Condensing the buildings onto ten acres would leave forty acres for agriculture. Purchasing the fifty acres located on the highway would allow us to build a safe children's village and a self-sustainable community center. One day, the project would be run entirely by Liberians.

During the rest of our time in Monrovia, we connected with our other pastor friend who leads a church, school, and orphanage for some much-needed advice. We did some shopping, played with our friends at the orphanage again, and returned to Buchanan with a clear vision. We walked around the perimeter of the land and continued the discussions we had begun in Monrovia. We quickly met with the landowners, committed to purchasing the property from them, and gave ourselves plenty of time to raise the needed funds. By now in this faith journey, we knew that God could do the impossible. While $30,000 was a large amount of money for fifty acres, it was also only $30,000 for fifty acres. The price per acre was $600, and we only needed fifty people, churches, or businesses to sponsor an acre to meet the goal before the end of the six-month deadline that had been set.

With a clear commitment and a vision in place, we could not wait to return home and invite others into this next turn of the story. Instead of being the end of our ride together, it seemed we had entered only the beginning. We trusted that God would continue to guide each step of our way as we stepped out in faith again. On our way home from Liberia, I sent a quick text to a friend and fellow adoptive parent:

"If we thought adoption and starting Psalm 82:3 Mission was a roller coaster, I am pretty sure we just left kiddy-land and got in line for the adult rides."

CHAPTER 10

UNEXPECTED BLESSINGS

uthor Mike Yaconelli wrote a book in 2000 called, *Dangerous Wonder: The Adventure of Childlike Faith.* In the book, he states, "Christianity is not about learning how to live within the lines; Christianity is about the joy of coloring." Through the stories of the Bible, God extends an invitation for His people to find Him in the faith of a child, from Moses witnessing the plagues to Jesus and His disciples living each day like a new adventure of curiosity.

In September 2017, a new vision was born for Psalm 82:3 Mission. A team of four people returned home with boxes organized on a sheet of paper, phases to accomplish a vision, and a list of potential people to get involved. We returned home believing that God was going to turn fifty acres of land into a safe children's village and self-sustainable community center in Grand Bassa County, Liberia, Africa. To participate in any part of what would happen was well beyond our own abilities, talents, or resources. We had barely learned how to connect sponsors to children and would now have to trust God in greater ways than we had until this point. We would continue to do this as volunteers so that all funds given would go directly to the ministry in Liberia.

We began to meet with any person, church, or business that would consider joining us as a $600 one-time partner so that we could purchase the land for $30,000. We hired our friend, the assistant director from the orphanage in Monrovia, to become our project manager for the new endeavor. Then we made plans for our first fundraising banquet to be held in December. The focus would always remain on orphans, but the first steps of the new vision included purchasing and clearing part of the land.

On a snowy day in December 2017, we gathered with nearly two hundred people to tell stories, bid on auction items, and celebrate what we believed God was going to do. Due to the weather, several were unable to attend. A few were so determined to attend that they arrived more than an hour late. Many of the people in attendance were past Psalm 82:3 Mission team members, making the banquet like a sweet reunion of short-term missionaries. Our new project manager joined us from Liberia and others who came had been previous donors or were invited by partners. Two partners had decided beforehand to give very generous gifts, and by the end of the night, the $30,000 needed to purchase the land had been given. In fact, the funds given surpassed the need! It was time to get to work.

At nearly every circus and carnival is a juggler: a person with a unique talent to keep multiple things like fire, balls, or even swords in the air. When I was a child, I joined the clown ministry at our church. A few times each year, we would travel to places like a nursing home to perform and bring smiles. No matter how hard I tried, I could never master the art of juggling. The moment a second item would be added, everything would come crashing down. To succeed at juggling, a person must maintain focus. The reality in my mind was that one day, I would begin to drop or fail at opportunities, and eventually everything would come crashing down.

With the funds raised, a few more steps were needed to purchase the land. Official documents in Liberia were needed for the deed, corner markers were identified, and a non-profit organization (Non-Government Organization—NGO) was created in Liberia: Psalm 82:3 Mission Liberia. We purchased a truck for the ministry, and our project manager relocated from Monrovia to Buchanan. Three team members planned to travel in April, and at the request of our Liberian partners, Psalm 82:3 Mission began serving in the community in partnership with a couple of orphanages and by meeting basic needs in nearby villages.

New church partners joined as a part of their own faith journey. These churches varied in size and demographics. It was clear that God was going to include who He wanted in this story for His children. One church, hoping to climb out of a steep debt, included Psalm 82:3 Mission as a two-year partner. They called their program Cannonball as they made a huge splash, both locally and globally.

In April 2018, Terah, myself, and a new mission team member journeyed to Liberia to finalize the purchase. Again, we held a revival service with the local pastor, connected with our friends at the old orphanage, made many plans, and held a huge community meeting in a makeshift tent on the land. We also had a couple of beautiful moments to pray with some of our old buddies from the orphanage as they prepared to travel home to America with their adoptive families. One of the families was a couple adopting three children. The other family was a single mother adopting two girls. It was a joy to play and pray with both families, but when we arrived to see the mother and her daughters, the older child ran to us and jumped into our arms for a huge hug. It was so great to know that, even though our partnership had ended with the orphanage, the relationships were still woven tightly together.

While we were in Liberia, we learned that our church back home had made the decision to do a major remodel in the kids' area and my role would soon change from elementary ministry to preteen ministry. The project and role change were both what we had wanted and were something we had been hoping would happen for a couple of years. When we returned from Liberia, the remodel began. Through the tireless effort of more than fifty volunteers, walls were removed, walls were built, painting was done, and carpets were cleaned, all in less than a month. A couple of weeks after the completion, we held Vacation Bible School in the new space with more than a hundred children.

In June, another team traveled to Liberia to clear some land and oversee the building of a basic open-air shelter. A couple weeks after the shelter was complete and the mission team had returned, villagers surrounding the land began asking our project manager to start a church in the shelter. We learned that the villages in our new area were controlled by a secret society that still practiced female genital mutilation, child sacrifices, and, in large part, controlled those living there with fear and witchcraft. The desire of those asking for a church was to flee the secret society and its practices and to have a relationship with Jesus. With the help of our pastor friend, a church was soon started with weekly worship and Bible teaching. By the end of the summer, more than ten people had surrendered their lives to Jesus and been baptized.

Since the beginning of Psalm 82:3 Mission, there had been many moments of overlap between family, work, and missions as God worked out His story. With the change in ministry roles and the growth in Liberia, I was really starting to feel that there were more balls in the air than I could focus on. There was a danger that something was going to fall soon as we trusted God to keep the different things floating in the air longer.

In 2015, the Christian band 7eventh Time Down, released a song called, "God Is On The Move." The lyrics at the beginning of the song are:

. . . God is on the move, Hallelujah. God is on the move in many mighty ways.
God is on the move, on the move, Hallelujah. God
is on the move, on the move today. . . .[1]

In Liberia, a church had started. In our church ministry, a busy summer schedule with VBS, camps, and school partnerships was underway. In our personal lives, our oldest son was entering his eighth-grade year, our two

---

1 7eventh Time Down. "God is on the Move." BEC Recordings, 2015. Accessed 2022.

children from Liberia were entering fifth grade, and our youngest child was entering second grade.

Then, one day, we received an unusual text from our fellow adoption friend that had brought two children home to Lexington in October 2016. Our friend had learned about a situation for one of the children recently adopted from the orphanage. This was the same mother with the two daughters we had prayed with in April. The adoptive mother had made the decision to end the adoption of her older daughter. As soon as we heard about the situation, our minds were flooded with how this sweet girl had jumped into our arms in April when we saw her. Terah and I prayed. Then we called the mother to offer the option of a school year of respite. Respite is a temporary rest for children and families in foster care and adoption. When it was clear the decision had been made to end the adoption, we prayed some more. We sat down with our kids and asked them their thoughts. All four kids were open to the idea of bringing the child into our family. Our youngest son felt like this was why we had an extra seat in our van. Our oldest son was more logical and only requested that we move to a bigger house. We agreed.

With the school year approaching quickly, we prepared our house for sale and began looking at options to either build or relocate. We researched schooling options and determined that a smaller community than Lexington would provide the best opportunity for growth. Much to our surprise, God moved in other ways as well. Several friends gave generous gifts to cover airfare and future steps.

At the beginning of August 2018, Terah and I boarded a plane for Kansas to bring home our future daughter, Blessing. A couple of days later, when our plane landed in Lexington early in the morning, we were greeted by our other four children and our beautiful friends with their adoptive family. That same day, some other treasured friends stopped by so we could pray with them. We had met these friends when they became the directors of the church camp—the same camp at which many parts of this story had taken shape. These friends were on their way to the airport. They were traveling to Liberia to the same orphanage to finalize the adoption of their daughter.

Within a month, we sold the house we had lived in since 2010, brought Blessing home, and purchased our new home in a smaller community called Nicholasville. We even lived in our church's missionary house for a few weeks until we closed on our new home. God's blessings were clear throughout this time: our house sold for significantly more than we could have imagined, and our new house was the perfect place for our family to grow. As a special bonus, the day we closed on our new home and received the keys was also the day we traveled to the Lexington airport. At the airport, Blessing was the first friend to welcome her best friend home from Liberia. How sweet it is to see God's ability to weave stories together!

The rest of 2018 was a little blurry. Our family had suddenly grown to five children. We adjusted to our new community and focused on finalizing our third adoption. To do this included more home studies and applying for and receiving a grant for the adoption. Psalm 82:3 Mission continued to serve monthly needs in Liberian communities, and the church in the shelter continued to grow. New churches began to connect to the ministry throughout southern Indiana, Ohio, and Kentucky. One church even joined with us at the annual mission conference when they learned that we had started a church in Liberia and they loved supporting pastors. In the past, we had been involved with leading the children's area, but now we were hosting a booth space, reconnecting with past friends, and telling the story of what we believed God was going to do.

In November, Psalm 82:3 Mission held its Second Annual Banquet. The focus was to raise the funds necessary to build the first orphanage on the property in Liberia. My oldest brother, an architecture professor, became a part of the story by designing the first orphanage home as a template for future structures. Our project manager from Liberia joined us again in Lexington. Generous gifts were given, including our first matching challenge. Auction items were sold. God provided.

A few weeks after the banquet, the small team in Buchanan began to prepare for an enormous Christmas celebration. It would be our first community Christmas. Plans and details had been worked out for the past several months and everything was in place. Hundreds of people would be served and, more importantly, the birth of Christ would be known. The night before the event, tragedy struck the ministry for the first time in Liberia. We had experienced plenty of setbacks but never tragedy. Earlier in the day, our new head of security had collected his first payment and had taken it home to his family. That night, as he was walking across the highway to start his shift, he was struck by an oncoming car. The team did everything they could to help him. They rushed him to the nearest medical facility and then transferred him to the capital city for treatment. As the team waited for answers to prayers, they returned to the mission to start the Christmas celebration. Just as they reached the mission, they received a call that, despite the best efforts of the staff and the medical team, the young man had lost his life. He left behind his children and a fiancé.

The staff was devastated, but they remained committed. The message of hope to the world would be shared with hundreds while, at the same time, comfort was given to a few. The tragic loss of this man deepened our resolve. The orphanage would hopefully be built in 2019 and God was indeed on the move.

CHAPTER 11

TRUST AND OBEY

n 1887, a man named John H. Sammis wrote a hymn called "Trust and Obey." The refrain of the song states, "Trust and obey, for there's no other way, to be happy in Jesus, but to trust and obey." Neither are easy, but both are necessary in the faith journey.

The first few months of 2019 were focused on allowing our personal lives to work out, developing a preteen ministry, and making plans for the next steps in Liberia. Blessing would officially become a Lee in April, our family would enter the world of raising teens, and my wife would return to teach in the elementary schools after twelve years staying at home with our children. My focus at the church was now on 4th–8th graders. This age group of students asked similar questions, loved adventures, and were never afraid to try crazy things like baking treats for the homeless or walking around a community asking for prayer requests. In an odd way, it was as if I had now been given the opportunity to lead the age group of students with whom I connected best. In Liberia, the church would continue to grow, our team would begin building the orphanage, and we would make plans for agriculture.

In February, the small staff team in Liberia gathered for a ground-breaking ceremony for the orphanage. The celebration was as large as the dream of helping many children find healing and hope. Hundreds of people attended the celebration. The land was prayed over and dedicated with oil, and construction was quickly underway. The goal was that, by January 2020, the home would be opened and serving children full-time.

After church one Sunday in March, I received a call from my younger sister that began a snowball effect of changes for Psalm 82:3 Mission. My sister told me about a deep sensing that God had placed on her heart to serve in Liberia for one year with her three children. I was excited to have her connected to this story, but secretly felt as if God had dialed the wrong number. The need for her to serve was great, but sending my sister and her kids to one of the poorest countries on earth for a year was more than my faith could grasp. She committed to prayer and fasting for clear direction while the Lord and I had some serious conversations about His plans versus mine. After her time of prayer and fasting, she believed even more strongly in this call to serve as the first on-ground missionary for Psalm 82:3 Mission. Her urgency to get to Liberia was both inspiring and frightening. Together, we set a goal to get her on the ground by September with many steps, trainings, and connections needed in between.

During our connecting to others already serving in Liberia, a partnership between missionaries grew using social media. At first, the partnership was focused on helping my sister navigate life in Liberia and only included those in our most direct area. Quickly, the message group extended to missionaries across the country and became the private group, "Christians for Liberia Partnerships." Since it began in 2019, the group has now grown to more than one hundred missionaries and organizations. The discussions and topics range from spiritual challenges to new items found in markets. It is open to all groups that refer to themselves as Christians and have a reach around the globe. There have even been moments that lives have been saved as the body of Christ has worked together.

Toward the end of March, a church we had connected to several times in the past called me with an unusual request. In the beginning, our relationship was more like an annual reunion that connected our churches at summer camp. As the relationship grew, the children's ministries partnered together for special family events called Rescue Nights using a guide for baptism called "The Rescue Manual." Eventually, these relationships grew into adoptive families working together. This phone call was very different. This call was an invitation to partner the church with Psalm 82:3 Mission.

The following week, I sat down with the staff of the church. Psalm 82:3 Mission had a lot of goals as we took steps toward the main vision in Liberia. I shared about three main areas of focus coming up and an estimated cost for each area. The total for all three areas would be nearly $30,000. I left hoping they would possibly choose at least one area. A couple hours later, the church informed me they were going to do all three. The following Sunday, the staff shared the idea with their church family, and within a few weeks, the goal was surpassed. Meeting this goal kicked off another faith step for their church and deepened our partnership together.

Many things were happening at the same time for Psalm 82:3 Mission as we entered the summer months of 2019. Several churches connected to the ministry in unique ways. Two mission teams were set to travel in June and July, and my sister's funding to be the first missionary was quickly taking root.

The purpose and method for each church fundraising was as unique as the church. One church in Indiana raised funds for goats by promising that every goat funded could be uniquely named. Oddly enough, the first "kids" on the mission were named Lieutenant Dan, Piper, and Joshua. To raise funds for a community playground, several churches joined together in their area for an annual community VBS. When they met their goal, the leader of the VBS promised to kiss a pig. . . . and he did. Other churches linked with Psalm 82:3 Mission through a "Mission March," allowing team members to share at their services, or even raising funds through a six-hour rocking chair challenge.

The first summer team was focused on learning more about agriculture options, building discussions, and interviewing potential staff. A team of three traveled first to Zambia to see a ministry partner's method in growing berries and to experience their focus on serving orphans and vulnerable children. The time in Zambia was less than thirty-six hours but included a new connection to another orphan-focused ministry and vast knowledge gained that shaped the future of our focus on foster care. In Liberia, the team joined up with my brother, the architect. He had designed buildings that, with a few changes, could significantly decrease the temperature of the home using wind funnels built into the exterior, an open concept, and facing the buildings in certain directions. We were excited to see that his research and style had already made a huge difference in the orphanage building under construction. Finally, we conducted many interviews as we prepared to hire orphanage staff, teachers, medical professionals, and a security team in the future.

The second mission team of six arrived in Liberia a few weeks later and gave great guidance to the next steps. It was a follow-up trip for a couple people from the 2012 remodel team and second trip for a very loving 78-year-old team member. The trip was the first for others, including a social worker, a man very familiar with agriculture, and my sister who was planning to move to Liberia. In just a few days, the team was able to lead the first trauma-healing training, build soccer goals, and develop a plan for the coming "kids" (goats). My sister was also able to locate the home she would live in by connecting to new missionary friends.

When I was in college, I took an intro to art class. On a fall day, the professor directed our class outside with pencil and paper and required each of us to identify one thing to stare at for an undetermined amount of time. The challenge was to stare at the item we had chosen for as long as needed to identify the finest details. As a person who loves nature, I went off to a quieter place, leaned against a tree, and picked up a recently fallen leaf. At first, I could see the outer edge of the leaf and the midrib, the part that feeds to both sides of the leaf from the stem. I drew these parts on my paper and continued to stare. Soon, I was able to see things that I had paid little attention to before. Every part of the leaf had veins connecting it together. It was in the details that the beauty of the leaf took shape.

Through God's faithful provision, my sister and her three children moved to Liberia in early September 2019. They had completed all required trainings, and their funding was in place. Their home church, a used car business, and several generous supporters provided the funding they needed. From the beginning of their journey to the end of their one-year commitment, their church and private school followed closely.

As my sister and her children discovered their unique reasons for being in Liberia, several other changes also took place. Through a global push to decrease long-term care facilities for children called orphanages, the government of Liberia challenged us to focus on foster care. Foster care is a less-permanent solution that aligned with some of our hopes. In caring for orphans and vulnerable children, we desired to first reunify with a family and, as a last result, maintain the option for adoption for all children. This change was exciting and allowed us to be only the second ministry in the entire country of Liberia focused on foster care.

With the future foster home quickly taking shape, it was important for other projects and plans to be completed as well. A large tower was built for water access and connected to a 150-foot borehole well with a submersible pump. A security wall was built around the current space, and a security team was officially begun to keep the future children safe. Finally, a permanent driveway onto the property was built into the plans.

In early October, at the church on ground, my sister and her Liberian driver noticed that several children attended but were not engaged in the church services. A couple weeks later, they decided to try children's ministry for the first time with a handful of children in a Bible study. The following week, more than thirty children attended the children's class. Two weeks later, more than seventy children were attending. Within a couple months, the group of children now walking from several villages ranged in age from one to thirteen and had grown to 130 children. The only place they could meet was in the kitchen space of the future children's home, but it did not seem to matter where they were meeting. Their only interest was in learning more about Jesus, having a special place for their age group, playing games, and eating some snacks after church.

Finally, a third mission team traveled to Liberia. This team consisted of a photographer, a pastor, and another of my brothers. My brother, a doctor, had been to Liberia with the 2012 orphanage remodel team as the lead electrician. The focus of this smaller team's journey was to experience what was happening in their own way and to return to their church family, the church in Cincinnati, ready to tell stories that would deepen their commitment as a partner.

From the moment I began in children's and youth ministry, one question was a constant: "When will you become a real minister?" In the early years of full-time ministry, this question was received as an insult to the hard work and dedication of my position. As time went on, it felt as if my passion and ability to connect with children and preteens had waned after almost twenty years of leading them in ministry. Though I loved doing preteen ministry, maybe it was time to trust God in new challenges and ways.

Entering the final quarter of 2019 meant another large fundraising banquet for Psalm 82:3 Mission, preparation for an upcoming mission trip, and an agriculture missionary was planning to join the team in Liberia. It meant closing out the year in preteen ministry with special events and Christmas celebrations. It meant finishing strong in the year nearly behind us and looking forward to 2020.

The fundraising banquet was focused on raising the funds necessary to build a missionary house and staff house on the property, completing the future foster home project, and equipping a growing children's ministry in Liberia. More than 100 people gathered for the banquet, many generous gifts were given, silent auction items were sold, and more than $50,000 was raised.

While everything happening was exciting, it seemed there was something else stirring in our personal, ministry, and mission lives. I began having discussions with several people about the possibility of focusing on planting a church in our area. A future church would have a large emphasis on the mission in Liberia while being dedicated to the mission of the church locally. As conversations developed, it was very clear that this was not our path forward.

Each week, our project manager and I would go over some updates about the mission. During one of our calls, a long pause of silence filled the air. For the past year, he had been married to a young lady from Liberia that now lived in the United States. They hoped to start a family together, but to do this, his family needed to be a higher priority. By the end of the call, a decision had been made that our faithful friend and partner, who had served at the orphanage and now led the team in Buchanan, would resign from his role as project manager at the end of the year. He had one project on his heart to complete before he left his role: the playground for the children in the community.

The change in Liberia's leadership opened my eyes to a new possibility forward. With a growing list of connected churches in the U.S., more staff, new leadership, the future foster home focused on girls between 3-10 years old, and missionaries on the ground, it was time to focus on Psalm 82:3 Mission full-time. There were a variety of reasons why our board had not made this decision before, but as things had progressed forward, this change had now become a necessity.

At the end of 2019, I began taking steps toward an exciting yet very challenging future. In late December, I resigned from full-time children's ministry with the hope of transitioning into the role of Executive Director of Psalm 82:3 Mission by April 1, 2020. The church was gracious and generous to allow me a lengthy time of transition, and even decided to pay me through May 2020.

The future ahead would be filled with new and exciting possibilities that would include learning to raise financial support for not just the mission but also to support our family with five growing children. The future ahead would include a lot of traveling but would allow me to focus on just one area of ministry. The future ahead was filled with great excitement and many unknowns. To move forward with what God had placed in front of us, we would have to trust Him again in ways deeper than we had before. God had carried us through so much before; it was time to trust Him again with the next steps of this journey.

A FEW MORE STEPS TO HOME

had already planned, briefly, for the downtown portion of the trail, as I figured this would be the hardest part. The river was too deep for us to swim, and again we would be going against the current. I made the decision that we would have to walk straight through downtown. I had to be careful, though. Chance wasn't shod—metal shoes for horses—and he jumped at every loud noise. This meant that, instead of taking the straight road through town, I needed to stay on quieter streets or, when possible, walk on sidewalks with me walking next to him. This would also allow him to rest from carrying my weight. As we walked through the downtown area, we passed a couple of people we knew, but we didn't stop to chat. I knew it was weird, but now—six hours in—Chance and I were going to make it home.

Going through downtown took longer than I had planned, of course, and our energy level was extremely low when we made it back to the highway that led nearly straight to our house. With too many semis driving by and lots of traffic, I chose to take a different straight path: the railroad tracks. Too rough on Chance's hooves for me to ride, I tossed the reigns over my shoulder and together we trudged forward. One foot in front of the other, stopping often to take breaks, but still going forward.

Another hour of walking the tracks, and my house finally came into view. With a newfound sense of purpose and energy, it felt like we had turned the corner to life's longest marathon and the finish line was now in sight. Nothing would stop us from making it home—nothing except a very curious state trooper. Through the blur of sweaty, tired eyes I could see an officer waiting for me a few hundred feet away. He had his lights on, but at least he was smiling. My feet and back hurt, but I chose to be respectful. We exchanged the normal greetings from a cowboy to a police officer, and I asked the obvious question.

"Sir, am I doing something wrong?"

His reply put me at ease. "No," he said with a small chuckle. "It's not every day I see a man walking his horse down the railroad tracks. I was just curious if you had a plan."

My reply that day was the same as it has always been when I think about it.

"Yes, sir," I said. "My plan is to make it home, and I have just a few more steps to get there."

"Therefore, since we are surrounded by such a great cloud of witnesses, let us throw off everything that hinders and the sin that so easily entangles. And let us run with perseverance the race marked out for us, fixing our eyes on Jesus, the pioneer and perfecter of faith. For the joy set before him he endured the cross, scorning its shame, and sat down at the right hand of the throne of God. Consider him who endured such opposition from sinners, so that you will not grow weary and lose heart" (Hebrews 12:1-3, NIV).

Chance and I eventually made it home that day, and in December 2021, Chance completed his journey at 26 years of age. Though he was a horse, he was also a great friend.

The journey of Psalm 82:3 Mission continues to take steps to develop a safe children's village and self-sustainable community center in Liberia, Africa. Each day, lives are impacted through foster care, church and community, medical care, education, and employment. The commitment to defend the weak and fatherless deepens daily as one of the poorest places on planet earth becomes a place of hope, healing, and brighter futures. To learn more about how to get involved in Psalm 82:3 Mission, go to psalm823.org or contact me directly at 859-537-2634.

Keep going friend. Fix your eyes on Jesus, and remember . . . just a few more steps to home.